# Bulimia Nervosa and Binge-Eating

# BULIMIA NERVOSA & BINGE-EATING

## A Guide to Recovery

Peter J. Cooper

NEW YORK UNIVERSITY PRESS
Washington Square, New York

First published in the U.S.A. by
New York University Press
Washington Square, New York
Copyright © Peter J. Cooper 1993, 1995
Reprinted 1996

**Library of Congress Cataloging-in-Publication Data**

Cooper, Peter J.
Bulimia nervosa & binge-eating:
a guide to recovery/Peter J. Cooper
p. cm.
ISBN 0-8147-1522-2
ISBN 0-8147-1523-0(pbk)
1. Bulimia-Popular works. I. Title.
RC552.B84C67 1995
616.85'263-dc20                95-8359
                                CIP

Printed and bound in Great Britain

# Contents

# Acknowledgments

The self-help manual which forms the major part of this book is based on the application of cognitive behavior therapy to bulimia nervosa and binge-eating. This application was first described by Dr Christopher Fairburn of the Department of Psychiatry at the University of Oxford in 1981 in an article in the journal *Psychological Medicine*. Over the course of the subsequent fifteen years, I have worked with Dr Fairburn and his colleagues to develop and refine this method of treatment, and I am enormously indebted to Dr Fairburn for his advice and support in modifying the treatment program so that it can be presented in the form of a self-help manual.

The manual as it appears in this book has gone through a great many revisions. These have been motivated largely by the comments and criticisms I have received from people with bulimia nervosa who have been using the manual as a means to recovery. I am very grateful to them for their help in shaping the final version. I am particularly grateful to those people who have agreed to my including in this book direct quotations from their accounts of their problems, and of their use of the manual.

A number of my colleagues have been kind enough to read the manuscript of this book and offer advice and criticism. For this service I am especially grateful to Sarah Beglin, Sian Coker, Carmel Fleming, Lynne Murray, Jane Steere and Christina Wood.

Finally, I am indebted to Tamara Hug for the help she gave me in the work which has culminated in this book.

P.J.C.

# Preface

The main aim of this book is to give people with bulimia nervosa and binge-eating problems the means to help themselves towards recovery. To this end the core of it (Part Two) consists of a self-help manual, which sets out detailed guidelines about what steps need to be taken to restore control to one's eating. These guidelines are based on extensive research into the most effective means of treating people with bulimia nervosa.

The self-help manual as presented here has gone through many revisions. These have been made on the basis of the experience of myself and my colleagues in helping patients with bulimia nervosa use the manual. A great many of these patients have now done so and gained considerable benefit from it. It is clear that the great majority of people with bulimia nervosa and binge-eating problems could effectively use the principles spelled out in this manual as a guide towards recovery.

It is important to be clear about what 'recovery' from bulimia nervosa means. Many people do recover fully. They become able to eat normally without anxiety and without the concerns about their weight and shape which used to dominate their lives. However, many remain vulnerable to difficulties with food and related concerns, even if that vulnerability only becomes evident on rare occasions of stress. The existence of this residual susceptibility does not mean, however, that the person has not recovered. Indeed, a realistic notion of recovery that accepts that difficulties with eating may occasionally recur is both more sensible and more helpful than a rigid definition, and can be protection against both disappointment and imprudence.

## Preface

This book is principally intended for people with bulimia nervosa and variations of this disorder. However, it will be of use to some other people as well. The families and friends of people who binge often want to know more about the problem. Part One provides a brief account of the nature of bulimia nervosa and binge-eating problems which will be of use to them, as well as a note on the definition of bulimia nervosa and binge-eating and its relation to other eating disorders. Also, it is helpful to someone who is trying to use this manual if other people in their household are aware of what they are trying to do. By reading the manual, a parent, partner or friend can ensure that they give as much help as possible. Finally, it is suggested in the self-help manual that it is advisable for the person wishing to use it to recruit the assistance of a helper. This could be a friend or relative, but it is preferable if it is someone less closely involved with them, such as a general practitioner, a nurse or a dietitian. Clearly, for such a person to be of most help, they too need to know what advice is contained in the manual.

January 1995

*Note*:
Since the second edition of this book is to appear in both America and Great Britain and the Commonwealth, 'mid-Atlantic' style has been adopted.

# PART ONE

# About Binge-Eating
# and Bulimia Nervosa

# Prologue

## 'A Day in My Life'

'I wake up late. It is a quarter past eleven and I have missed my morning classes. I feel terrible. My head aches. My mouth feels dry. My throat is sore. My eyes are puffy. And my face feels swollen. I get out of bed and almost faint I am so dizzy. Remembering last night's binge-eating and vomiting, I feel so ashamed and disgusted with myself. Why do I do it? I go to the bathroom and get on the scales. I do this three times just to make sure. 127 pounds. I have gained two pounds since yesterday. This is terrible.

'Today I shall have to make sure I eat absolutely nothing. I have three glasses of water and feel a little better, resolved to fast for the entire day. I consider having a bath but shower instead so that I will not have to look at my thighs spreading out before me. I decide that I am too fat to go out. I pad round my room doing a little tidying and trying to write a letter to my mother. But I can't stick at anything. All I can think about is how fat I am. At a quarter past two I weigh myself again. Three times. 126 pounds. Hooray!

'I drop in on a friend. She is in the kitchen. I join her and, when she offers me a cracker, I have one. I have two more. I am feeling very nervous now because I should not have eaten anything. I excuse myself, go to the toilet, drink water from the tap, and stick my fingers down my throat and get rid of the crackers. I feel better but still a little shaky because I think I am hungry. Thoughts of food go round and round in my head.

'I decide it was a mistake to come out and head back to my room. On the way I pass the bakery. In a moment the urge to binge sweeps over me and my resolve crumbles. I buy two Danish pastries, a cheese roll, three doughnuts and, round the corner, two chocolate bars and a large bottle of lemonade. I rush up to my room, spread the lot out before me. I start eating. At first the taste and texture of the pastry is wonderful. I feel thrilled and appalled at the same time. I eat very fast. I drink the lemonade straight from the bottle to wash down the food. I just shovel it in, not tasting it at all. In 20 minutes it has all gone. I feel uncomfortably full. If I try to move I feel a sharp pain in my stomach. I try not to look down because I am aware that my stomach is sticking out.

'I go to the toilet, stick my finger down my throat and vomit. I do this again and again to make sure I get rid of as much of the food as possible. I go to my bed and lie down. All I can think about is that I have gained more weight. I try to calm down but this is impossible and I go and weigh myself. 128 pounds. I feel in despair. I go back to my bed, lie down and cry. I hate myself. I hate my fat body. I am so disgusting.

'I doze for a while. When I wake up I feel I must eat. It is night. I go to the corner shop. I feel as if I am almost in a trance. I buy more food. Chocolates, bread, a pack of cereal. Thankfully nobody knows me around here. I return to my room and eat the lot. I vomit again. I feel terrible. I cry myself to sleep.'

# 1

# What Are Binge-Eating and Bulimia Nervosa?

*'I began binge-eating when I was about seventeen. I was lonely, shy and lacking in self-esteem. Every binge made me feel worse, made me hate myself more. I punished myself with more and more food. Within months I was binge-eating as a matter of course, and I gained weight rapidly. I loathed myself and only continued with normal life by pretending to be "normal".'*

Almost everyone at some time or other overeats. It is common for people to regret such indiscretions and to feel a little guilty and ashamed about them. Such episodes and feelings are so common that they are perfectly 'normal' and not a source of concern. For others there is a very different quality to their overeating. They would say, with deep shame and remorse, that they lose control of their eating and binge.

Binges are by no means the province of people who are overweight. Indeed, about half those with the eating disorder anorexia nervosa, who are by definition very thin, experience episodes of binge-eating. And some whose weight is within the usual range also binge. Many of these have an eating disorder which has come to be known as bulimia nervosa. In addition to binge-eating, these people go to great lengths to compensate for overeating and are intensely concerned about their body shape and weight.

## Binge-Eating

### What is a Binge?

*'It starts off with me thinking about the food that I deny myself when I am dieting. This soon changes into a strong desire to eat. First of all it is a relief and a comfort to eat, and I feel quite high. But then I can't stop and I binge. I eat and eat frantically until I am absolutely full. Afterwards I feel so guilty and angry with myself.'*

The word 'binge' is used differently by different people. It has taken some time for a consistent definition to be established, but over the past few years a clinical consensus has emerged. It is now accepted that a true binge is an episode of eating marked by two particular features. First, the amount eaten is, by 'normal' standards, excessively large. Second, the eating is accompanied by a subjective sense of loss of control.

### The Experience of Binge-Eating

*'I randomly grab whatever food I can and push it into my mouth, sometimes not even chewing it. But then I start feeling guilty and frightened as my stomach begins to ache and my temperature rises. It is only when I feel really ill that I stop eating.'*

Binges almost always occur in secret. Indeed, this secret can be kept for many years. The binges take place in private and, often, an appearance of 'normal' eating is maintained in front of others. Keeping this secret can involve considerable subterfuge and deception.

Binges typically take place where food supplies are kept, often the kitchen. Some people binge while buying food, eating between shops.

*'I leave work and go shopping for food. I begin eating before I get home, but it is secret, with the food hidden in my pockets. Once I'm home proper eating begins. I eat until my stomach hurts and I cannot eat any more. It is only at this point that I snap out of my trance and think about what I have done.'*

Usually, the food eaten in a binge is consumed very quickly. It is stuffed into the mouth almost mechanically and barely chewed. The first moments of a binge are often described as pleasurable; but soon all sense of taste and pleasure is lost. Many people drink large quantities during binges, which contributes to their feeling progressively full and bloated.

'When the urge to binge comes I feel hot and clammy. My mind goes blank, and I automatically move towards food. I eat really quickly, as if I'm afraid that by eating slowly I will have too much time to think about what I am doing. I eat standing up or walking around. I often eat watching television or reading a magazine. This is all to prevent me from thinking, because thinking would mean facing up to what I am doing.'

Many people describe their binges as frenetic and desperate affairs. There is a powerful craving for food which they experience as overwhelming. It is this sense of being driven to eat which has led some to use the term 'compulsive eating' to describe binge-eating. The desperation people feel drives them to behave in ways quite alien to their character. They will take food belonging to their friends, steal from shops, or eat food that others have thrown away.

'I begin by having a bowl of cereal. I eat it really quickly and then immediately have two or three more bowls. By then I know that my control is blown and that I am going to go all the way and binge. I still feel very tense and I desperately search for food. These days this means running around college looking for food people have thrown out. I know that this is really disgusting. I stuff the food down quickly. Sometimes I go into town stopping at stores along the way. I only buy a little from each store so as not to arouse suspicion. I stop when I have run out of money or, more usually, because I am so full that I physically cannot eat any more.'

## What is Eaten, and How Much?

*'I stop eating when I begin to feel ill. By then I have an overwhelming desire to rid myself of all the food I have eaten. I push my finger down my throat and vomit again and again until I feel completely empty. This makes me feel relieved and cleansed. It also leaves me exhausted.'*

The amount eaten during a binge varies greatly from individual to individual. Occasionally a patient will describe regularly having binges of 20,000 calories or more. This is not typical. The average calorie content of a binge tends to be between 1,500 and 3,500 calories.

*'After a binge I feel so full that my stomach hurts and I can hardly move. I feel sick and sometimes, when I have had a particularly bad binge, even breathing is difficult and painful.'*

Some eating episodes which are not binges in terms of the definition given above are nevertheless seen as binges by people who experience them. Although these episodes do not involve the consumption of abnormally large amounts of food, they are nevertheless distressing because the person feels out of control and eats when she would prefer not to do so.* These 'binges' have been called 'subjective binges', to distinguish them from true 'objective binges'.

True binges typically consist of bulk foods which are filling and high in calories. They tend also to be foods that people regard as fattening and which they are attempting to exclude from their diet. Many people believe that binges are especially high in carbohydrates, and that binges are driven by a specific 'carbohydrate craving'. This view is mistaken. Compared to normal meals, binges do, indeed, contain more carbohydrate; but they also contain more fat and more protein. And the

---

* Because the majority of people who binge are women, female pronouns are used throughout this book to avoid the clumsiness of using both genders: 'he or she might feel', 'in his or her experience', etc. This is not in any way meant to exclude men.

proportion of a binge made up of carbohydrates is almost exactly the same as in normal meals.

*'The food I eat usually consists of all my "forbidden" foods: chocolate, cake, cookies, jam, condensed milk, cereal, and improvised sweet food like raw cake mixture. Food that is easy to eat. Food that doesn't need any preparation. I never eat these kinds of food normally because they are so fattening. But when I binge I can't get enough of them.'*

## What Triggers Binges?

Binges tend to be triggered by the same sort of events or experiences. These can be divided broadly into three categories:

(1) *Those concerned with food and eating, e.g.:*
    breaking a dietary rule;
    having 'dangerous' (i.e. 'fattening') foods available;
    feeling full after eating;
    thinking about food.

*'The urge to binge usually begins around midday on a "normal" day – that is, a day on which I am trying not to eat. During the afternoon thoughts of food become more and more of a preoccupation; and eventually at around 4.00 p.m. my power of concentration will be sufficiently non-existent for thoughts about food to be totally overwhelming. So I leave my work and go to the store.'*

*'One thing that definitely sets me off is hunger. If I am hungry, instead of eating something to satisfy it, I eat anything I can lay my hands on. It's almost as if I have to satisfy all tastes, even for things I don't like.'*

(2) *Those linked to concerns about body weight and shape, e.g.:*
    brooding about shape or weight;
    discovering weight to be higher than expected;
    feeling fat;
    discovering clothes to be too tight or too small.

'If I discover my weight has gone up, or I find that my clothes are too tight, or I look in the mirror and see that I am too fat, immediately I want to eat. I know this is silly when I really want so desperately to be thin, but I just feel as if I can't cope any more and I might as well just give up and eat. Of course, I feel even worse after the binge.'

(3) Negative mood states, e.g.:
    feeling miserable or depressed;
    feeling lonely or isolated;
    feeling tense, anxious or fearful;
    feeling angry or irritable.

'Binges start when I'm tired or depressed, or just upset. I become tense and panicky and feel very empty. I try to block out the urge to eat but it just grows stronger and stronger. The only way I know to release these feelings is to binge. And binge-eating does numb the upset feelings. It blots out whatever it was that was upsetting me. The trouble is that it is replaced with feeling stuffed and guilty and drained.'

All of these examples are reported as triggering binges by the majority of those who binge.

## How do People Feel after a Binge?

The feelings people have after binges are a complicated mixture of emotions. There is an immediate sense of relief at having given up the struggle not to eat; but this is soon replaced by feelings of shame, guilt and disgust. Depression is common after binges as people feel hopeless about ever being able to control their eating.

These feelings are made worse by the physical effects of binge-eating. Tiredness, abdominal pain, headaches and dizziness are common. Feelings of extreme fullness and bloatedness are almost always present. The fear of weight gain is acute and drives people to adopt extreme methods to compensate for having overeaten.

10

'*After a binge I feel agitated, annoyed and frightened. Fear is a large part of what I feel about my eating, especially when I am totally out of control and horribly alone. My stomach and back ache and I feel hot and panicky. I am terrified about the weight I have gained. I feel full of anger towards myself for allowing it to happen yet again. I feel unclean inside. Dirty. I don't want anyone to see me. I hate myself.*'

## Methods of Compensation

Many people who binge go to considerable lengths to compensate for their episodes of overeating. In fact, such compensation is a defining feature of bulimia nervosa (see page 47). These include strict dieting and fasting, making themselves vomit, and taking laxatives, diuretics and appetite suppressants ('diet pills').

### Dieting

Most people who binge are at the same time attempting to diet in order to lose weight. Dieting usually precedes the onset of binge-eating. But it is also an understandable response to binges, in that the fear of weight gain after a binge drives people to cut back on their eating.

There are basically three ways in which people diet in order to lose weight and all three are typical of the eating habits of people with bulimia nervosa. The first method is fasting: that is, not eating anything at all for long periods of time. The second method is to eat sparingly: that is, to try to restrict eating to a small number of calories each day. The third method is to avoid certain types of food because they are believed to be fattening or because they have been found to trigger binges. These 'trigger' foods are often described as 'forbidden', 'bad' or 'dangerous' foods.

All three of these methods of dieting actually *encourage* overeating; and thus the process of dieting becomes inextricably linked to the episodes of loss of control over eating. Dieting makes people vulnerable to binges by creating physiological and psychological pressures to eat. And, as we saw earlier when looking at what triggers a binge, for people who have 'forbidden

11

foods', breaking the rules they have set themselves and eating these foods frequently triggers binges.

## Vomiting

*'I started vomiting after eating too much chocolate one day. It seemed a brilliant way of staying thin without dieting. I could eat as much as I wanted and then get rid of it. It would be so much easier than all that dieting.'*

The great majority of people with bulimia nervosa compensate for overeating by making themselves vomit. This is done privately and in secret. Typically, vomiting is induced by sticking the fingers or another object down the throat to induce the gag reflex. About a quarter of people with bulimia nervosa who vomit have voluntary control over the gag reflex: that is, they are able to vomit at will simply by leaning forward or by pressing their hand on their stomach.

*'I first started vomiting as a way of eating what I liked, without feeling guilty and without putting on weight. Vomiting was surprisingly easy and I was pretty pleased with myself. It was only later that I realized what a problem it had become.'*

How often people with bulimia nervosa induce vomiting varies considerably. Some people vomit repeatedly throughout the day, vomiting after binges and after having eaten anything they regard as fattening. It is not uncommon for people to be vomiting ten times a day.

While some people vomit just once after a binge, others will do so repeatedly, sometimes for up to an hour. This process is physically and emotionally exhausting. Some use a flushing technique: they vomit, drink water, vomit again, drink again, and so on; and they repeat this process until the water returns clear and they feel confident that they have eliminated all the food they possibly can. This can be physically harmful (see chapter 3).

*'I eat until I literally cannot eat any more. Then, using my fingers, I make myself sick. Over the next half-hour, drinking water*

*between vomits, I purge all the food from my stomach. I then feel despondent, depressed, alone and desperately scared because I have lost control again. I feel physically terrible: exhausted, puffyeyed, dizzy, weak, and my throat hurts. I am also scared because I know it is dangerous.'*

Usually people begin to induce vomiting as a response to having lost control of their eating. They binge, are terrified of the potential effect on their weight and shape, and therefore make themselves vomit. Many people say that when they first discovered that they could vomit successfully after eating, they felt quite elated, because it seemed to them as if they could now eat what they liked without this affecting their weight. However, this elation is short-lived, because it soon becomes clear that, by removing the psychological and physical barriers restricting eating, vomiting actually encourages overeating. Also, the process of vomiting is easier following the consumption of large rather than small amounts of food; so the size of binges increases. Vomiting, therefore, leads to more frequent binge-eating, and to eating more and more in each binge episode.

Some people who binge established the habit of vomiting before starting to experience loss of control over eating. They have used vomiting on top of dieting as a method of weight control. People who do this often find that at first it seems to work; that is, that they lose some weight. However, soon the combination of weight loss and hunger drives them to overeat. They respond by further vomiting which in turn leads to more overeating.

Some people who find it difficult to vomit take additional substances to induce nausea 'chemically'. They may drink salt water, or occasionally domestic chemicals, such as shampoo. Others take syrup of ipecac. All these practices are dangerous and have a variety of toxic effects.

*'Over the past eight years I have repreatedly said to myself "This is going to be the last time that I throw up". At first I was not that bothered: I thought I could control it, if I chose to. But it soon became clear that it had control over me. Now stopping seems completely beyond my reach.'*

There are a number of reasons why vomiting should not be used as a means of weight control. First, it can be physically damaging, even dangerous (see chapter 3). Second, it can be just as damaging psychologically, with most people who do it suffering feelings of considerable shame and guilt. Third, it often becomes a habit which is difficult to break. Finally, it is not nearly as efficient at eliminating calories as those who do it tend to believe. In fact, while the majority of calories consumed in a binge are usually eliminated by vomiting, a significant proportion are absorbed. Given that binges frequently consist of large amounts of food, the number of calories absorbed can be considerable. For some people who binge and vomit frequently and attempt to fast between binges, their body weight is largely maintained by the calories they absorb from binges.

## Misusing Laxatives and Diuretics

*'I started taking laxatives because I was scared that because I was eating so much I would get fat really quickly. I thought that if I took laxatives all the food would go straight through me.'*

*'I read in a magazine about people using laxatives as a way of purging themselves. I'd tried vomiting but couldn't do it. So I went out and bought some laxatives and downed ten after every binge. I know deep down that they didn't really do anything to couteract the binge, but they made me feel empty and cleansed inside.'*

About one in five people with bulimia nervosa attempt to compensate for having binged by taking laxatives in the belief that the laxatives will reduce food absorption. In fact this is not so, because laxatives act on the lower portion of the gut and calories contained in the food eaten are absorbed higher up in the digestive system.

There are a number of complications associated with using laxatives as a method of weight control (see chapter 3). One of these is that, if laxatives are taken regularly, the body gets used to them and higher and higher doses are needed to produce an effect. Some people end up taking considerable quantities (up to 100 times the normal dose). Another complication is that the body responds to the taking of laxatives by retaining fluid. This leads to edema (water retention), which causes puffiness round the eyes and general swelling, especially around the wrists and ankles.

*'The hardest thing after a binge is waiting for the effects to die down. I hate feeling so useless and unable to do anything. Sometimes I feel I could literally rip open my stomach and pull out the garbage inside, the disgust and revulsion is so great. Failing that, laxatives are the next best thing.'*

Some people use diuretics ('water tablets') instead of, or in addition to, laxatives, as a means of reducing their weight. However, diuretics have no impact at all on body weight. The small effect they seem to have is solely due to fluid loss; and this 'weight loss' is rapidly reversed when, in response to dehydration, fluids are consumed.

## Other Methods of Compensation
The desire to compensate for overeating and to reduce weight is intense in people with bulimia nervosa. They will do whatever they feel is necessary to avoid eating and to deal with having eaten more than they had wished. Some people exercise excessively, perhaps for many hours every day. Some take appetite suppressants. There is no evidence to suggest that these drugs are an effective way of reducing the frequency of binge-eating.

## Attitudes to Weight and Shape

*'My confidence and feelings of self-worth are deeply rooted in the idea that I must be physically attractive, i.e., thin. When I put on weight, even one pound, I risk being unattractive, and I see my future as bleak and lonely. This thought fills me with despair, so I force myself to eat as little as possible.'*

For many people who binge and all of those with bulimia nervosa, concerns about body weight and shape have huge and particular significance. Their sense of self-worth depends above all on how they feel about their weight and shape; little else, if anything, figures even nearly as strongly in their judgments of themselves. Concerns about their shape and weight dominate their lives. Many are consumed by a powerful desire to lose weight and become thin. If they think they have gained weight or have become fat, they see this as a catastrophe and it has a profound effect on their lives. They feel deeply depressed, avoid company and give up attempting to control their eating. As a consequence they binge, become more depressed and fiercely attempt to renew their efforts to diet and lose weight. If, on the other hand, they find they have lost weight they can feel quite elated. Most are acutely sensitive to small changes in weight and shape which are, in truth, undetectable by ordinary means.

*'I am confident in many ways, yet I hate my body and can't bear to look at it. I feel bloated, wobbly and huge all over. This drives me to binge. My boyfriend loves me. Why can't I like myself?'*

*'I am obsessed with my weight. I weigh myself over and over again, sometimes up to fifteen times a day. At other times I am so disgusted with my body that I don't use the scales for weeks or months at a time.'*

It is these concerns, and the belief that self-worth depends on weight and shape, which drive the disturbed eating habits of people with bulimia nervosa. Thus, dieting follows quite logically from these beliefs. And, given these beliefs, it is understandable why extreme measures (such as vomiting) are seen as necessary if overeating has occurred. Indeed, many working on eating disorders consider that beliefs and values about weight and shape are the core disturbance in bulimia nervosa.

People with bulimia nervosa usually have a disturbance in their body image. This takes two forms. First, they commonly feel strongly dissatisfied with their body shape. Typically, despite their weight being perfectly "normal", they feel certain parts of their body (for example, the stomach, bottom and hips) to be too fat. This often causes great distress and spurs them on to more intense dieting. Second, they tend to overestimate their actual size: that is to say, they see their body as larger than it actually is. On top of this, they have an unrealistically small 'ideal' size.

Figure 1 shows the differences in how a group of patients with bulimia nervosa, and a group of normal weight students not suffering from the disorder, saw their existing and 'ideal' shape.

The top row of outlines shows how the sample of 'normal' weight students saw themselves. Outline A is a representation of an average weight, average height young woman. Outline B shows the average of the student's own estimate of their actual size: and it is apparent that it is slightly more (about 5 per cent more) than the actual average size (Outline A). Outline C shows the desired size of these students, which is some 10 per cent below their actual size. In other words, it is common for young women of 'normal' weight to want to be 10 per cent slimmer than they actually are. The bottom row of outlines shows the same information for the sample of patients with bulimia nervosa. They overestimated their actual size (Outline D) by, on average, nearly 20 per cent (Outline E); and their desired size (Outline F) was 25 per cent below their actual size. In other words, they saw themselves as substantially larger than they actually were; and they wanted to be significantly smaller than they were. Indeed, they wanted to be almost half the size they thought they were.

*'I cannot put into words how repulsed I am with my body. I wish it were possible to wear clothes that disguised one's shape completely. I cannot bear to look at my body and will have no mirrors in the house. I take showers instead of baths to avoid having to look at myself. I have not gone shopping for clothes for more than three years.'*

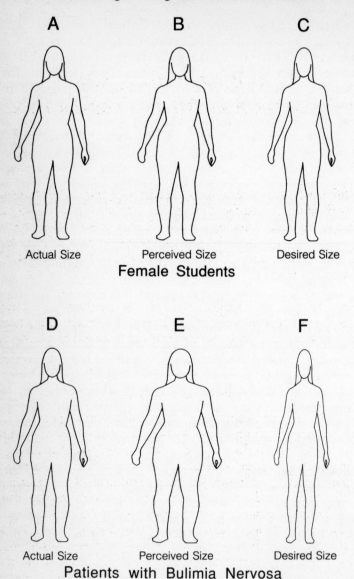

Figure 1   Actual, perceived and desired body size in people with bulimia nervosa and "normal" female undergraduate students

18

## 2

# How Binge-Eating and
# Bulimia Nervosa Affect People's Lives

'My life revolves around my eating. I can no longer concentrate on my work which has suffered greatly as a result. My problem has caused family rows. I no longer enjoy sharing meals with family or friends. I have become withdrawn and introspective and have lost all self-confidence and self-respect. I don't want to go out. I don't like myself any more.'

Bulimia nervosa and binge-eating have a profound effect on people's psychological well being and their social life. Symptoms of depression and anxiety are common and social life can suffer greatly.

## Symptoms of Depression

As noted in the previous section, the self-esteem of people who binge is intimately bound up with how they see their body shape and weight. So, if they regard their weight or shape to be unacceptable, they feel themselves to be worthless. Therefore, it is particularly humiliating for them periodically to lose control of their eating and overeat. They feel intensely ashamed of themselves and disgusted at themselves for being unable to maintain control over their eating. At times they feel utterly desolate and quite hopeless about their eating ever improving.

Not surprisingly, patients who binge who come for treatment typically display a number of symptoms of depression. Table 1 shows how often such symptoms occurred in one group of patients with bulimia nervosa. The figures in the table are based on patients' responses to a standardized psychiatric interview designed to detect the presence of symptoms of sufficient severity to have a marked negative effect on functioning.

It can be seen from the table that by far the majority of people with bulimia nervosa experience a wide range of depressive symptoms. Most of these symptoms relate directly to the core disturbances in eating and the patients' concerns about their shape and weight. So, the guilt which so many experience is usually rooted in shame about binge-eating and vomiting; the worthlessness stems from feelings of failure surrounding their control over their eating and their inability to achieve a weight and shape they regard as acceptable; and the loss of confidence and withdrawal from social contact result from feeling unable to eat in company and from regarding their shape and weight as socially unacceptable.

**Table 1** Symptoms of depression in a group of patients with bulimia nervosa

| Symptom | Frequency (%) |
| --- | --- |
| Feelings of guilt | 94 |
| Poor concentration | 80 |
| Feelings of worthlessness | 74 |
| Irritability | 71 |
| Lack of energy | 71 |
| Loss of self-confidence | 66 |
| Depressed mood | 63 |
| Social withdrawal | 63 |
| Feelings of hopelessness | 60 |

Many people who binge feel quite desperate at times. They hate what they are doing, they despise themselves, and they can see little, if any, prospect of their situation improving. In these circumstances, some attempt suicide, usually by taking an overdose of pills. Around 5 per cent of people with bulimia nervosa coming for treatment in Britain have at some time taken an overdose.

For the great majority of people who binge, once they have regained control over their eating habits, the depressive symptoms disappear. However, in a small minority there is a depressive disorder which is independent of the disturbance in eating. In these patients, even if their eating disorder improves, the depressive symptoms remain severe and disabling. It is important that these people, in addition to receiving help in overcoming their problems with eating, receive specific treatment for their depression.

## Symptoms of Anxiety

People who binge frequently report that they have distressing symptoms of anxiety. These include the mental symptoms of worrying and anxious foreboding, as well as physical symptoms such as palpitations, sweating, difficulty in breathing and churning of the stomach. Table 2 shows how often some of these symptoms occurred in a group of patients with bulimia nervosa. As in table 1, the percentages show how many patients experienced these symptoms severely enough to have a marked effect on their lives.

**Table 2** Symptoms of anxiety in a group of patients with bulimia nervosa

| Symptom | Frequency (%) |
| --- | --- |
| Worrying | 69 |
| Tension pains (e.g. tension headaches) | 68 |
| Nervous tension (i.e. keyed up, on edge) | 68 |
| Active avoidance of anxiety-provoking situations | 62 |
| Anxiety when meeting people | 51 |
| Anxiety in specific situations | 48 |
| Panic attacks | 10 |

As with depressive symptoms in people who binge, these anxiety symptoms are closely linked to the core disorder of eating. So their worrying tends mainly to be focused on their concerns about food, eating, shape and weight; and the situations in which they become anxious, and which they avoid, are those where there is food around or where they would feel particularly fat. These anxiety symptoms only rarely require separate treatment from the eating problems. That is, if the eating disorder is brought under control, the anxiety tends to lift spontaneously.

## Anger

Many people who binge, at times when they have done things they regret, such as following a binge, feel extremely angry with themselves. Some people take laxatives after a binge explicitly for their unpleasant physical effects, as a means of self-punishment. Others punish themselves even more drastically. Some will hit themselves with a belt or rope or even knock themselves about with a hammer. Others cut themselves. Usually the cutting or scratching causes only minor skin wounds, with some bleeding. In some cases, however, the cutting is much more serious, with deep wounds being made into the muscle. People cut themselves for two reasons. First, it is a violent expression of anger and a direct form of punishment. Second, for some people, it is used to release tension, either as the urge to binge builds up or else following a binge.

## The Effects on Social Life

'My eating problem has taken over my whole life. My friendships have been upset by my violent swings in mood. I never talk to my parents since they have never understood what I am going through, yet we were so close. I have so little self-confidence. I get terribly depressed and anxious. I can't face seeing people.'

The personal and social lives of people who binge suffer considerably. As already noted, binge-eating is largely a secretive practice. And the extreme measures to which people go to compensate for overeating, like vomiting and taking laxatives, are usually a source of much guilt and shame. This causes many people to keep their disturbed eating habits a complete secret for a number of years. This has the effect of isolating them, because a central part of their existence is kept hidden away from those with whom they live and otherwise share their lives. It is for this reason that binge-eating is a particularly lonely activity.

Concerns about shape and weight have a direct effect on social functioning. It is common for people with bulimia nervosa only to mix socially when they feel reasonably happy about their weight and shape; but the moment they binge or feel they have gained weight or become fat, they withdraw completely. Some will literally hide away, refusing to see anyone, or to allow anyone to see them, for days at a time.

Much of ordinary social life takes place around food and eating. Friends meet in bars or restaurants. They invite each other to their homes for meals. And families gather together around the table both routinely and for special occasions. All of these ordinary situations create difficulties for someone who binges; and in some, they evoke terror. The typical response is to try to avoid these situations altogether. As a consequence, they cut themselves off from 'normal' social life.

Bulimia nervosa and binge-eating can take a considerable toll on family life. The partner of someone with this disorder is exposed to rapid swings in mood as control over eating is maintained and then lost. Partners are frequently at the receiving end of marked irritability, and their social life is at the mercy of the course of their partner's eating disorder. Children can suffer in much the same way. And, of course, family meals are a source of special difficulty to people who binge.

A major concern for people who binge, especially for those who are doing so often, is how to finance their eating habits. Binge-eating can be extremely expensive and leads many people into debt. Some, as already noted, much to their shame, find themselves taking food belonging to others. And some steal food and other items from shops in order to indulge their binges. This can lead to considerable friction with friends and relatives; and, of course, it sometimes leads to prosecution in the courts.

The social and personal lives of people who binge are transformed when they recover from the disorder. So much of ordinary life which had previously been closed to them is opened up by their being able to socialize freely. Intimate personal relationships become much easier and more fulfilling. And family life becomes much happier.

# 3

# The Physical Complications

Bulimia nervosa and binge-eating bring with them a number of physical complications. These arise either as a direct result of binge-eating or as a consequence of the measures taken to compensate for overeating.

## The Physical Effects of Binge-Eating

Binges usually produce a sense of fullness and bloatedness; sometimes this is so extreme as to cause profound abdominal discomfort and, occasionally, acute pain in the abdomen. The fullness frequently leads to breathlessness caused by the distended stomach pressing up against the diaphragm and thereby interfering with breathing. In rare cases, the stomach wall can be damaged and even tear. This is a serious medical emergency.

General digestive problems are common among people who binge. These include stomach cramps, flatulence, constipation and diarrhea.

## The Physical Effects of Methods of Compensation

*Dieting*
Dieting can have adverse physical effects. It has been suggested that repeatedly going on and off diets (so-called 'yo-yo dieting') can actually cause people to gain weight over time. What seems to happen is that, when they are dieting and losing weight, their bodies become metabolically efficient and they can function on a

relatively low number of calories without losing weight. Then, when they resume eating normally (or begin overeating) this metabolic efficiency persists and they gain weight rapidly, overshooting the weight at which they started dieting. This would explain why people who go on and off diets tend gradually to become heavier and heavier.

Both a low carbohydrate diet and a low body weight can have a significant impact on hormonal functioning. Menstrual periods may become irregular or stop altogether. This is because normal menstruation depends on the body maintaining a certain proportion of fat (around 20 per cent). The dieting practised by people with bulimia nervosa often reduces the proportion of body fat to below this critical level. It has also been found that a woman who is only 5–10 per cent under her ideal body weight may undergo subtle alterations in the menstrual cycle which can cause infertility.

*Self-induced Vomiting*
As noted above, vomiting is not nearly as effective a means of compensating for overeating as people tend to believe. It also has a number of adverse physical effects, some of which can be medically serious.

First, repeated vomiting leads to an erosion of the dental enamel, mainly on the inner surface of the teeth. This is caused by the teeth repeatedly being exposed to acid from the stomach. Many people brush their teeth vigorously after vomiting to get rid of the smell; this actually damages the teeth further, because the presence of the acid in the mouth means that brushing the teeth effectively scours them. Using a mouth wash, rather than brushing, would reduce the potential damage somewhat. However, the damage caused to the teeth by repeated vomiting is irreversible.

Second, vomiting causes the salivary glands below the jaw to swell. This is painless, but it does make the face look rather puffy; this is particularly distressing to someone with bulimia nervosa, who is apt to interpret the swelling as a sign of weight gain and may well respond with further vomiting.

Third, repeated vomiting often causes damage to the throat. This is because most people who vomit need to induce the gag reflex by sticking something down their throat. Gagging in this way is sometimes difficult and some people have to use considerable force. The back of the throat is frequently injured in this process. Sometimes it bleeds and the injuries often become infected. People who vomit frequently commonly develop a hoarseness in their voice.

Very rarely, violent vomiting causes a tear in the esophagus (the tube linking the mouth to the stomach). If the esophagus ruptures, it is a medical emergency. Vomiting repeatedly for many years can also lead to a weakening of the esophageal sphincter (the set of muscles at the top of the stomach). The result of this is that there is nothing to prevent the contents of the stomach from returning up the esophagus into the mouth (so-called gastric reflux). This can be uncomfortable, distressing and embarrassing.

The effects of vomiting on the body's physiology can be serious, especially for those who flush their stomachs by repeatedly vomiting, drinking and vomiting again until they are satisfied that their stomach is empty of food. This process upsets the balance of body fluids and body salts (electrolytes). The abnormality of most concern is low potassium (hypokalemia) because it can result in serious heartbeat irregularities. Almost half of those with bulimia nervosa who come for treatment have some fluid or electrolyte abnormality, but most of these will not show any symptoms. Electrolyte disturbance is reversible and the abnormalities disappear once vomiting stops.

## Misusing Laxatives and Diuretics
As noted above, laxatives and diuretics, like vomiting, are ineffective as well as a dangerous way of attempting to control weight. Laxatives have very little impact on calorie absorption, and diuretics have none at all. Misuse of laxatives causes several complications. As already mentioned, people may become dependent on them and need to take larger and larger doses to achieve the desired effect. Also, stopping taking laxatives can be difficult, because the shock to the body that has become used to them leads to 'rebound' constipation and water retention. The latter effect can also arise when people stop taking diuretics.

As with vomiting, laxative and diuretic misuse can cause a variety of fluid and electrolyte abnormalities. People who both vomit and take laxatives are especially at risk of such complications. Some laxatives, when taken in large doses, can cause damage to the gut wall. However, the other physical consequences of laxative and diuretic misuse disappear rapidly once the person stops taking them.

*Appetite Suppressants*
There is no evidence that appetite suppressants have a significant impact on binge-eating. They also have certain complications; for example, they can cause agitation or depression. They cannot be recommended for people who binge.

Most people who come for treatment of bulimia nervosa or binge-eating have been overeating and vomiting for some years. By this time many will have suffered some damage to their teeth. However, they are most unlikely to have caused themselves any other permanent physical harm. When they restore their eating habits to normal their bodies soon return to a healthy state.

# 4

# What Causes Binge-Eating and Bulimia Nervosa?

*'I had been anorexic for about a year and was attempting to start eating properly. One day, out of the blue, I ate a chocolate cookie. Suddenly I began eating all these things I'd deprived myself of. It wasn't a large binge by my current standards, but it was more calories than I normally ate in a whole week. I came out of my trance-like state and was suddenly terrified about what I had done. I immediately went to the bathroom and stuck my fingers down my throat. I had to throw up and get rid of all the garbage inside me.'*

Understanding the causes of any illness, be it psychiatric or physical, is a complicated process. This is because the causes of medical conditions are rarely simple. Tuberculosis is a good example from physical medicine. It can, quite rightly, be said to be caused by infection of the lung by the tubercle bacillus. However, a number of factors other than exposure to the bacillus are also relevant to whether or not someone actually develops tuberculosis. So, certain people are more prone to infection if exposed, such as the infirm and the undernourished, and those with a genetic predisposition to the disease; and some are more likely than others to go into physical decline once they have become infected, such as the elderly and those with weak physiological defenses. The causes of psychological problems such as depression, anxiety and eating disorders are even more complicated, and that much more difficult to understand.

It is helpful when trying to understand the causes of a disorder, to divide up the various factors into those which make people vulnerable to the disorder ('predisposing factors'), those which bring on the disorder ('precipitating factors') and those which, once the disorder has become established, maintain it or prevent sufferers from recovering spontaneously ('maintaining factors').

The causes of binge-eating and bulimia nervosa have not been well studied and they are poorly understood. Nonetheless, it is clear that the disorder arises from the interaction of physical, psychological and social factors. The relative importance of these various factors in causing a person to develop binge-eating or bulimia nervosa varies from one individual to another. In the rest of this chapter these three sorts of factors will be discussed in terms of what makes a person prone to develop bulimia nervosa and binge-eating, what can actually bring it on, and what makes it continue.

## What Makes a Person Vulnerable to Binge-Eating and Bulimia Nervosa?

*Physical Factors*

It is possible that a tendency towards eating disorders may be in part inherited. Two types of evidence support this view. First, eating disorders run in families. Second, in cases where one of a pair of twins has an eating disorder, if the twins are identical (that is, share the same genes) rather than non-identical, it is much more likely that the other twin will also have an eating disorder. Both of these findings could arise because a tendency to develop eating disorders is passed on from parent to child in the genes. However, on the other hand, both of these facts could also be explained in terms of the family environment rather than in terms of physical heredity. Family members, after all, to a large degree share the same environment; and it could be this common experience that explains why eating disorders run in families. Again, identical twins are likely to share the same environment to a greater extent than non-identical twins, and it may be this, rather than shared genes, that accounts for the high occurrence of eating disorders in both of a pair of identical twins.

30

Depression is common among the family members of people with eating disorders; and about a third of those with eating disorders have themselves experienced an episode of depression before the onset of their eating disorder. These facts have led to the suggestion that an inherited tendency to depression raises the risk of someone developing an eating disorder. However, the way in which being prone to depression might raise the risk of eating disorders is not at all clear. Also, the relationship between family depression and eating disorder could be explained in psychological rather than physical terms. That is, having a depressed parent might produce circumstances which raise the chances of having low self-esteem, which might then make one vulnerable to the development of an eating disorder.

Finally, inheritance might contribute to causing binge-eating and bulimia nervosa in terms of the genetic transmission of body weight. There is good evidence that there is a major inherited component to how much one weighs as an adult. Many people who binge have a tendency to have a higher than average natural weight. Indeed, nearly half of those with bulimia nervosa have been significantly overweight before the onset of their eating problems. This suggests that a tendency to be overweight makes a person vulnerable to the development of bulimia nervosa and binge-eating. Such a tendency might contribute to the onset of eating problems when combined with some of the psychological and social factors that we shall now look at.

*Psychological Factors*
About a third of those who develop bulimia nervosa do so following an episode of anorexia nervosa. Some may lose control of their eating following a period where they have successfully restricted their calorie intake; as a consequence, their weight rises. For others, binge-eating may have always been part of their anorexia nervosa; but at some point the frequency and size of binges increase and they gain weight.

The precise way in which anorexia nervosa raises the risk of bulimia nervosa is not known. It might be largely physical; for example, it may be the starvation state itself which leads to binge-eating. Or the chain of cause and effect might be

31

psychological: for example, dieting and preoccupations with food may raise the risk of episodes of loss of control. Or a combination of physical and psychological factors might be involved.

Certain psychological characteristics appear to make people vulnerable to developing an eating disorder. Low self-esteem and a profound sense of ineffectiveness commonly precede the onset of eating problems. In some cases these difficulties appear to relate to early trauma, such as an unhappy family. About a third of people with bulimia nervosa report having been sexually abused. This fact has led some to conclude that childhood sexual abuse is a specific cause of eating disorders. However, this is not the case, because childhood sexual abuse is just as commonly reported by people with other psychiatric disorders such as depression but without eating problems. While such abuse is clearly detrimental to children's psychological development, it does not appear to lead to a specific type of disorder.

People who develop eating disorders often have a tendency towards perfectionism. They set very high standards for themselves and strive assiduously to meet their goals. Some authorities argue that it is the combination of perfectionism and the sense of ineffectiveness described above which is the major factor predisposing people to develop eating disorders.

A history of problems with alcohol has also been found to be a predisposing factor to the development of an eating disorder.

*Social Factors*
Binge-eating and bulimia nervosa only occur in certain cultures; and it is almost exclusively confined to women. This suggests that social factors are important in predisposing some people to the development of eating disorders. This view is supported by the observation that eating disorders are especially common in certain social groups such as ballet dancers and fashion models. It is striking that what these groups have in common is a strong emphasis on the desirability of thinness. Indeed, it has been suggested that changes in fashion over the years have contributed to the recent increase in the incidence

of eating disorders. Fashion models have become progressively thinner in recent decades and at the same time eating disorders have become more widespread. There is no way of telling for certain whether this association is a purely accidental one. But it certainly might not be. If the presentation of thin fashion models in the media increases the number of girls and women who go on diets, then it is highly probable that the changes in fashion which have occurred in recent years have been responsible for more women dieting and, therefore, more women developing eating disorders.

In fact, the current fashion industry projects an image of women which is positively unhealthy. A recent article in the *British Medical Journal* has observed from a study of fashion mannequins that these models are so thin that, if they were flesh and blood, they would fail to menstruate! A number of feminist writers have argued persuasively that the pressures women are under to be thin are a tyranny which they should fiercely resist.

Finally, there are social factors which operate within the family which may predispose some people to develop eating disorders. For example, concerns about shape and weight may be transmitted from mothers to their daughters. Certainly, the daughters of women who diet are highly likely to diet themselves. In addition, people with eating disorders describe their family relationships as much more disturbed than do people with no psychiatric problems. However, it is uncertain whether these relationship difficulties precede the onset of the eating problems or arise as a consequence of them.[1]

## What Brings on Binge-Eating and Bulimia Nervosa?

*Physical Factors*
Some cases of binge-eating and bulimia nervosa arise after weight loss following an episode of physical illness. This weight loss might invite positive comment from friends and evoke a

[1] A good account of the contribution of social factors to the causation of eating disorders is given by Richard Gordon in his book, *Anorexia and Bulimia: Anatomy of a Social Epidemic*, Blackwell Publishers, Cambridge, Mass., 1993.

sense of accomplishment and social acceptability. In this context, the desire to diet in order to prevent weight gain is a powerful one.

*Psychological Factors*
The single most important precipitating factor in binge-eating and bulimia nervosa is a period of dieting. The great majority of those who binge can recall clearly a period of dieting, which may or may not have led to weight loss, preceding the first occasion on which they lost control over their eating. And herein lies a paradox. It would be expected that people with extreme concerns about their shape and weight would respond to minor infringements of their dietary rules by more stringent dieting. However, people who binge respond to small dietary indiscretions by abandoning altogether their efforts at dieting, and overeating instead. On the basis of this paradoxical response of people who diet and binge, some have argued that it is the dieting itself which actually causes the episodes of loss of control. This argument certainly fits with the accounts that people with bulimia nervosa themselves give. It is also consistent with certain laboratory studies of how people who diet eat. For example, if people who are not dieting drink a high-calorie milk shake (a so-called 'preload') and then are asked to rate the taste and texture of certain foods, they will eat smaller amounts of those foods in order to make their ratings than they would if they had not had the milk shake. People who are dieting, on the other hand, behave in exactly the opposite way: they will eat more in the tasting session if they have had a high-calorie 'preload' before the session than if they had not had one. This paradoxical way of behaving by dieters has been called 'counter-regulation'.

This counter-regulation effect is illustrated pictorially in figure 2. It is interesting that this effect arises in dieters following various provocations other than a high-calorie 'preload' – including simply believing they have had a high-calorie drink, even if, in fact, the drink contained few calories. This strongly suggests that the effect is driven by psychological factors rather than by physiological ones. Other factors which have been found to produce the counter-regulation effect in dieters are depressed mood and the consumption of alcohol. What these provocation factors appear to have in common is that they undermine a dieter's resolve to resist eating.

The counter-regulation effect found in laboratory studies of dieters has been presented as an analogy for what is happening in people who binge. As an analogy it is illuminating; and, certainly, people who do lose control of their eating will identify with what is happening in figure 2. However, although dieting does appear to be important in setting off binge-eating, it is not at all clear why, among the great number of people who diet, some lose control of their eating and others do not.

Some people who binge are adamant that they were not dieting before they began to lose control over eating. In these people, binge-eating appears to have served a particular psychological function. They may have overeaten in response to stress;

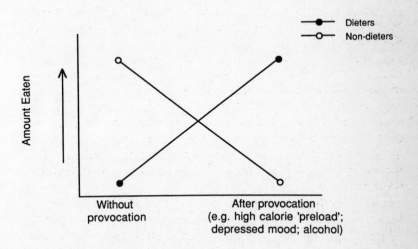

Figure 2   Schematic representation of the 'counter-regulation' effect

or they may have used eating as a way of blotting out unacceptable feelings of misery or anger.

*Social Factors*
In some people who binge a social situation or experience has clearly provoked the disturbed eating habits. For example, a woman might describe being rejected by a potential boyfriend or being teased about being fat, and having started dieting as a result. Other people describe friends going on a diet and joining in to conform. Many people can identify social circumstances like these which precipitated their dieting; and they clearly identify this as the beginning of their problems with eating. However, few can recount social factors directly relevant to the onset of their binge-eating.

## What Keeps the Vicious Circle Going?

*Physical Factors*
Being significantly below one's natural or healthy body weight serves to perpetuate eating disorders. This occurs through a number of physical and psychological mechanisms. A low weight leads to preoccupation with food and eating. It also causes depressive symptoms; and these in turn damage self-esteem further, leading to social withdrawal and a reduction in outside interests, including, sometimes, a loss of interest in sex. All these changes increase social isolation and remove the stabilizing influence of ordinary social life.

A low body weight also places the body under physiological pressures to eat, regardless of the cause of the weight loss. There has been clear evidence of binge-eating among men and women under starvation conditions. When body weight falls too low, the normal physiological processes operating to control eating appear to be disrupted. Such a disruption can contribute to the perpetuation of binge-eating in people who weigh significantly less than they are biologically meant to weigh.

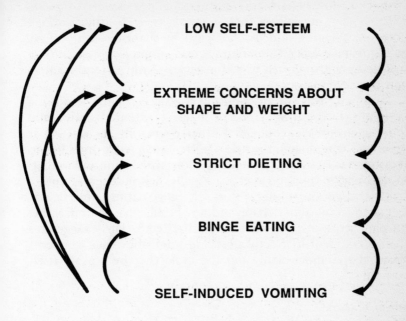

Figure 3 The psychological factors that serve to maintain bulimia nervosa
*Source*: Adapted from C. G. Fairburn and P. J. Cooper, 'Eating Disorders', in K. Hawton, P. Salkovskis, J. Kirk and D. M. Clark, eds, *Cognitive Behaviour Therapy for Psychiatric Problems: A Practical Guide*, Oxford, Oxford University Press, 1989.

*Psychological Factors*
A number of psychological factors serve to perpetuate binge-eating. Those that operate in maintaining bulimia nervosa are illustrated in figure 3. Look first at the downward arrows on the right-hand side of the figure. At the root of bulimia nervosa, as we have already seen, is a profound lack of self-esteem. This leads, in vulnerable people (e.g., those with a tendency to be overweight in a society where slimness in women is perceived as

essential to social success), to extreme concerns about shape and weight. These concerns drive the vulnerable people to go on strict diets. The dieting then encourages overeating, through both physiological and psychological mechanisms. The binge-eating in turn leads to extreme action adopted to compensate for the overeating, such as self-induced vomiting (and laxative and diuretic misuse).

Turning to the upward-pointing arrows on the left-hand side of figure 3, vomiting (and, to a lesser extent, laxative and diuretic misuse) encourages further overeating, because it is perceived as removing the need to attempt to resist urges to eat. It also serves to heighten preoccupations with shape and weight, as do binge-eating and dieting. Finally, self-induced vomiting (and laxative and diuretic misuse), binge-eating and the extreme concerns about shape and weight all serve to undermine people's sense of self-control and self-esteem. This exaggerates their feelings of ineffectiveness and intensifies their concerns about shape and weight, and the cycle thereby repeats itself perpetually.

*Social Factors*
In many respects, the beliefs and values of people with bulimia nervosa about the importance of shape and weight are reinforced by the norms of Western society. There is a huge amount of advertising in women's magazines, on television, and so on, all of which glorifies female thinness and encourages the view that for a woman to be thin is a marker of success. It is difficult, against this tide of propaganda, for anyone to sustain the argument that body shape and weight are not really important. In this sense, our culture serves to encourage preoccupations with shape and weight in women, and it rewards successful dieting.

# 5

# *How Can Binge-Eating and Bulimia Nervosa Be Treated?*

Over the course of the 1980s there was considerable interest in developing and evaluating treatments for bulimia nervosa. This work proceeded in two main directions. First, a number of clinical researchers, mostly Americans, investigated the role of certain medicines, especially antidepressant drugs. Second, certain psychological treatments were developed, principally in Britain, and their effectiveness was assessed in clinical studies.

It is probably true that what we know about the treatment of bulimia nervosa also applies to people with other binge-eating problems. However, not enough research has been done to be sure about this. The rest of this chapter focuses on what we do know from studies of the treatment of bulimia nervosa. More information on the treatment of general eating problems can be obtained from an excellent new book by Christopher Fairburn, *Overcoming Binge Eating*, (Guilford Press, New York, 1995).

### The Main Types of Treatment

*Antidepressant Drugs*
The effectiveness of a number of antidepressant drugs in the treatment of bulimia nervosa has been assessed. These drugs come from three pharmacological groups: first, the monoamine oxidase inhibitors (such as phenelzine); second, the tricyclic antidepressants (such as imipramine, desipramine and amitriptyline); and third, the new generation of antidepressants, the serotonin reuptake inhibitors (such as fluoxetine and fluvoxamine).

The findings from the studies of antidepressant treatment of bulimia nervosa do show that patients benefit. The frequency of binge-eating decreases by, on average, 50–60 per cent within a few weeks of starting a course of treatment. And there is a corresponding decrease in the frequency of vomiting and laxative-taking. In addition, preoccupation with food and eating decreases and mood improves.

These findings look encouraging. However, recent research has revealed some serious limitations to this form of treatment:

(1) Although most patients who take antidepressant drugs do binge less often, few actually stop binge-eating altogether. While someone who reduces the frequency of binges from four times a day to twice a day could be said to be 50 per cent better, her eating habits could not be said to be 'normal' and she remains in need of help.

(2) Antidepressants have no impact on patients' tendency to diet. Since the strict dieting of people with bulimia nervosa is a major reason why they tend to binge, this is a serious limitation.

(3) Finally, and most significantly, recent evidence has revealed that, in many cases, the positive effects of antidepressants on binge-eating do not last. Many people who have experienced an initial benefit from antidepressant treatment later relapse, whether they continue taking the medication or not.

A further problem with treatment by medication is that many people with bulimia nervosa are reluctant to accept it. They want to tackle their eating problems on their own, without relying on a drug.

As it has come to be realized recently that antidepressant medication has only a limited impact on the longer-term outcome of bulimia nervosa, enthusiasm for this form of treatment has declined. It is particularly fortunate, therefore, that while the research into drug treatment has been taking place, similar work has been going on concerned with the effectiveness of psychological forms of treatment.

*Psychological Treatments*

*Cognitive behavior therapy* The psychological treatment which has attracted most interest is a short-term psychotherapy, known as cognitive behavior therapy, specifically designed for patients with bulimia nervosa. It is based on the view, for which there is considerable support, that a key factor which prevents people with bulimia nervosa from spontaneously recovering is their extreme concerns about shape and weight. The treatment aims to help people regain control over their eating and to moderate their concerns about their shape and weight. It is usually conducted on a one-to-one basis with patients seen around 20 times over the course of approximately five months.

The effectiveness of cognitive behavior therapy in cases of bulimia nervosa has been studied in a number of careful clinical trials. The short-term results are very impressive, with reductions in the frequency of binge-eating of, on average, around 90 per cent being achieved. Following a course of this treatment, approximately two-thirds of patients are no longer binge-eating. Vomiting and laxative-taking similarly decrease, and there is also a marked improvement in mood. Importantly, the tendency to diet is significantly reduced with this form of treatment. And patients' concerns about shape and weight become much less intense.

There are as yet few data on the longer-term impact of cognitive behavior therapy for bulimia nervosa. However, evidence is accumulating that the positive short-term benefits are well maintained: that is, the changes brought about by treatment do seem to be permanent.

*Other treatments* Many people who come for treatment of bulimia nervosa have had previous psychotherapy which has been unsuccessful. However, there are forms of psychological treatment other than cognitive behavior therapy which have been shown to be of some benefit to some patients with bulimia nervosa. None of these treatments is more effective than cognitive behavior therapy; most are less effective. They include

41

behavior therapy, psychoeducational treatments, and focal psychotherapies (such as 'interpersonal psychotherapy' and 'supportive-expressive therapy').

Two variations of these different types of treatment are sometimes advocated. The first involves giving a psychological treatment to a group of patients collectively. This method of treatment has not been well studied. However, it appears that it is somewhat less effective than individual therapy. Also, many people with eating disorders are too sensitive about their eating habits and their appearance to accept the idea of being treated together with other people. The second variation is a combination of a psychological treatment and an antidepressant drug. Again, this has not been well studied. Clearly, given the positive benefits of a cognitive behavioral approach, such combination treatment is, by and large, unnecessary. However, there are circumstances where such an approach might have benefits. One such circumstance is discussed in the next section.

## Treatment by 'Stepped Care'

People with bulimia nervosa and related problems differ in how much help they need to overcome their problems with eating. Some people will be able to recover completely on their own, with no outside help at all. Some will need to be admitted as inpatients to a specialist hospital unit. Most, however, will need a degree of help somewhere in between these two extremes. One sensible suggestion which has been made is that services for people with binge-eating problems should be organized in a 'stepped' fashion: that is, people would begin receiving the lowest level of care and move up the system, progressively receiving more intensive levels of care if and when they needed to. Opinions differ about precisely what services should be offered at each level. Figure 4 is an adaptation of a stepped care program recently proposed by the Royal College of Psychiatrists.

The first level is a system of supervised self-help. At this level people receive a self-help manual which they use under the

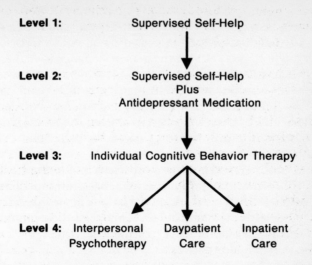

Figure 4  A stepped care program for the treatment of bulimia nervosa

supervision of a helper.* The supervision of this level could come from any one of a number of sources. In Britain doctors and the nurses who work with them are best placed to deliver this level of treatment. Social workers, psychiatric nurses and dietitians could also fulfil this role.

The majority of people with binge-eating problems will be able to make sufficient progress at Level 1 to require no further help. For those who do not make sufficient progress, further treatment will be necessary. There is uncertainty about what the next level of treatment should be. In figure 4, the second level of treatment involves continuing with the self-help manual while receiving antidepressant medication. There is, as yet, no good evidence to support this level of treatment. However, the reason why it might be appropriate is that the anti-bulimic properties of antidepressants could provide some people with the impetus they need to make use of the self-help manual. They may have

* Part Two of this book is a self-help manual designed to perform the function of Level 1 treatment.

the added benefit, in those who are significantly depressed, of improving mood. Since the benefits of antidepressants to people with bulimia nervosa have been shown to be only short-term, they are used here solely to give the person a chance to make use of the self-help manual.

Some people will not be able to manage to make sufficient progress even with the support of drugs; and some will not want to take medication. They will need to receive the next level of treatment, namely a full course of cognitive behavioral treatment.

The few people who do not make sufficient progress at Level 3 tend to be those in whom bulimia nervosa constitutes just one of many difficulties. They need additional help. The precise nature of this help depends on a detailed assessment of their problems as well as the availability of local treatment resources. Figure 4 gives three possible alternatives.

# 6

# A Short Technical Note

This chapter contains a brief account of how bulimia nervosa came to be recognized as a disorder, the prevalence of the condition, the criteria which have been specified for its diagnosis, and its relation to other eating disorders.

## How Bulimia Nervosa Came to be Recognized

It has been recognized for a great many years that disorders of eating occur which are essentially psychological in nature. The most well known of these is anorexia nervosa. The first description of a patient with this disorder was provided as long ago as 1694 by the English physician Richard Morton. He described the condition of a young girl, 'a skeleton clad only in skin'. The term 'anorexia nervosa' was introduced into the medical literature much later, in 1874, by Sir William Gull, Physician Extraordinary to Queen Victoria. There has, for a long time, been wide agreement about what the key features of anorexia nervosa are. Table 3 shows the definition recently provided in the diagnostic manual of the American Psychiatric Association.

Towards the end of the 1970s reports began to emerge of a new eating disorder in which the principal disturbance was episodes of uncontrolled overeating. People with this disorder were reported closely to resemble people with anorexia nervosa, except that they tended to be of 'normal' weight.

This newly recognized disorder was given a number of names (such as 'bulimarexia' and 'the dietary chaos syndrome'), but the two terms which gained widest acceptance were 'bulimia' (used

# About Binge-Eating and Bulimia Nervosa

in America) and 'bulimia nervosa'. The latter term was introduced by Professor Russell in a seminal paper which he published in 1979 in the psychiatric journal *Psychological Medicine*. In it he described the clinical condition of 30 patients suffering from 'an ominous variant of anorexia nervosa', a disorder he termed 'bulimia nervosa'. Professor Russell's paper is a remarkable exposition in which the features of a previously undescribed disorder are unfolded on the basis of the sensitive clinical observation of an experienced clinician. The paper is probably the most influential journal article to have been published in the field of eating disorders.

**Table 3**   The defining features of anorexia nervosa

A   Refusal to maintain body weight at or above a minimally 'normal' weight for age and height (e.g., weight loss leading to maintenance of body weight less than 85% of that expected); or failure to make expected weight gain during period of growth (leading to body weight less than 85% of that expected).

B   Intense fear of gaining weight or becoming fat, even though underweight.

C   Disturbance in the way in which one's body weight or shape is experienced, undue influence of body shape and weight on self-evaluation, or denial of the seriousness of the current low body weight.

D   In postmenarcheal females, absence of at least three consecutive menstrual cycles. (A woman is considered to have amenorrhea if her periods occur only following hormone, e.g., estrogen, administration.)

*Specific type:*

Restricting type
   During the current episode of Anorexia Nervosa, the person has not regularly engaged in binge-eating or purging (i.e., self-induced vomiting or the misuse of laxatives, diuretics or enemas).
Binge-Eating/Purging type
   During the current episode of Anorexia Nervosa the person has regularly engaged in binge-eating or purging (i.e., self-induced vomiting or the misuse of laxatives, diuretics or enemas).

# A *Short Technical Note*

## The Definition of Bulimia Nervosa

Professor Russell originally proposed the following three-part definition of the disorder bulimia nervosa:

(1) powerful and intractable urges to overeat;
(2) attempts to avoid the 'fattening' effects of food by inducing vomiting, abusing purgatives, or both; and
(3) a morbid fear of fatness.

Over the course of the next few years, this definition was widely used by clinicians and researchers, especially in Britain and the Commonwealth, in identifying people with this disorder. Unfortunately, the criteria used to define the disorder 'bulimia', specified in 1980 by the American Psychiatric Association, were far broader than Russell's. This led to some confusion in the medical literature, particularly in relation to estimates of how widespread bulimia nervosa was (see below). However, agreement about the factors which define a case of bulimia nervosa has now been reached. Table 4 shows the latest formulation presented by the American Psychiatric Association. (The term 'bulimia nervosa' is now accepted on both sides of the Atlantic.)

Point A defines a binge as an episode of uncontrolled overeating. Point B lists a range of extreme methods used to compensate for overeating. Point C states that, for the disorder to be diagnosed, the disturbed eating habits should have been present for at least three months and have been occurring quite frequently. Point D states that a defining feature of the disorder is that self-evaluation is unduly influenced by body shape or weight. And point E states that, if all the four previous criteria have been met and the person also meets the criteria for a diagnosis of anorexia nervosa, then the latter diagnosis should take precedence. To aid future research into the disorder two sub-groups have been proposed, with a division between those who purge (vomit or take laxatives or diuretics) and those who do not.

**Table 4** The defining features of bulimia nervosa

A  Recurrent episodes of binge-eating. An episode of binge-eating is characterized by both of the following:
  (1)  eating, in a discrete period of time (e.g., within any two-hour period), an amount of food that is definitely larger than most people would eat during a similar period of time;
  (2)  a sense of lack of control over eating during the episode (e.g., a feeling that one cannot stop eating or control what or how much one is eating).

B  Recurrent inappropriate compensatory behavior in order to prevent weight gain, such as: self-induced vomiting; misuse of laxatives, diuretics or other medications; fasting; or excessive exercise.

C  The binge-eating and inappropriate compensatory behaviors both occur, on average, at least twice a week for 3 months.

D  Self-evaluation is unduly influenced by body shape and weight.

E  The disturbance does not occur exclusively during episodes of Anorexia Nervosa.

*Specify type:*

Purging type
  During the current episode of Bulimia Nervosa, the person has regularly engaged in self-induced vomiting or the misuse of laxatives, diuretics, or enemas.
Nonpurging type
  During the current episode of Bulimia Nervosa, the person has used other inappropriate compensatory behaviors, such as fasting or excessive exercise, but has not regularly engaged in self-induced vomiting or the misuse of laxatives, diuretics, or enemas.

# How Widespread is Bulimia Nervosa?

Since the publication of Professor Russell's 1979 paper and the appearance of the American criteria for bulimia in 1980, a number of studies have been conducted designed to determine the prevalence of bulimia or bulimia nervosa. Widely differing findings were reported. These related, in part, to the different definitions of the disorder being used. But they also related to the fact that key terms were not being adequately defined. For example, studies in which American college students completed questionnaires which asked if they ever binged reported that the rate of binge-eating was as high as 70 per cent. Similar studies in Britain, however, which inquired whether people ever experienced episodes of uncontrolled overeating, produced a figure of around 20 per cent for young adult women. In fact, when people are interviewed in detail about their eating habits, and a strict definition of a binge is applied, the prevalence of binge-eating among young adult women is between 5 and 10 per cent; and the prevalence of the full disorder of bulimia nervosa within this group is between 1 and 2 per cent.

Bulimia nervosa is rare among men.

The age at which bulimia nervosa begins is typically around 18 years, although most people who come for treatment do so in their early twenties. The disorder does occasionally arise in girls aged 13 and 14, but very rarely in girls any younger than this.

Over the past 20 years, bulimia nervosa appears to have become much more common. It is, however, not possible to be absolutely certain about this, because cases of this disorder may have existed previously but gone undetected. Studies have shown that a history of having had bulimia nervosa is much more common among younger than older women, which does suggest that the disorder has become more common in recent years. It is certainly the case that in countries where anorexia nervosa is found (i.e. Western and economically developed non-Western countries) there has, in recent years, been a dramatic rise in the number of people with bulimia nervosa coming for treatment. Indeed, bulimia nervosa is now one of the most common disorders encountered in outpatient psychiatric clinics.

## Bulimia Nervosa and other Eating Disorders

Bulimia nervosa is closely related to anorexia nervosa. About a third of those with bulimia nervosa have had anorexia nervosa in the past; and many more have had some of the features of anorexia nervosa. The two disorders also have many symptoms in common. In particular, they share a particular kind of attitude towards body shape and weight (see point C of table 3 and point

49

D of table 4). It is clear from the diagnostic criteria listed in tables 3 and 4 that it is possible for someone to satisfy the main four criteria for bulimia nervosa and also fulfil the criteria for a diagnosis of anorexia nervosa. Indeed, nearly half those who suffer from anorexia nervosa periodically lose control over their eating and binge. In recent years it has become increasingly recognized that there are people who binge but do not take any steps to compensate for overeating. It has been proposed that they should be classed as having a third type of eating disorder, termed 'binge-eating disorder'.

The proposed definition of binge-eating disorder is shown in table 5. More information on binge-eating disorder can be found in Christopher Fairburn's book *Overcoming Binge Eating*.

Figure 5 shows how the three types of eating disorder relate to one another. The size of the circles roughly corresponds to the relative frequency with which each occurs. The overlapping of the circles shows which diagnosis takes priority. There is a general rule in psychiatry that if someone is suffering from two disorders, then the one that has the greater significance for treatment and outcome 'trumps' the other one, that is, it takes

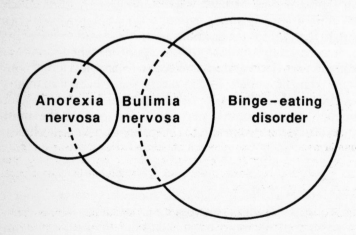

Figure 5    The relationship between anorexia nervosa, bulimia nervosa and binge-eating disorder

precedence in diagnosis and treatment. (See point E of table 4.)
According to this rule, a diagnosis of anorexia nervosa would
trump one of bulimia nervosa, and a diagnosis of bulimia
nervosa would trump one of binge-eating disorder.

**Table 5**  Defining features of binge-eating disorder

A   Recurrent episodes of binge-eating. An episode of binge-eating is
characterized by both of the following:
   (1)   eating, in a discrete period of time (e.g., within any 2-hour
period), an amount of food that is definitely larger than most
people would eat in a similar period of time under similar
circumstances:
   (2)   a sense of lack of control over eating during the episode (e.g., a
feeling that one cannot stop eating or control what or how much
one is eating).

B   The binge-eating episodes are associated with three (or more) of the
following:
   (1)   eating much more rapidly than normal;
   (2)   eating until feeling uncomfortably full;
   (3)   eating large amounts of food when not feeling physically
hungry;
   (4)   eating alone because of being embarrassed by how much one is
eating;
   (5)   feeling disgusted with oneself, depressed, or very guilty after
overeating.

C   Marked distress regarding binge-eating is present.

D   The binge-eating occurs, on average, at least 2 days a week for 6
months.

**Note**:   The method of determining frequency differs from that used for
bulimia nervosa; future research should address whether the pre-
ferred method of setting a frequency threshold is counting the
number of days on which binges occur or couting the number of
episodes of binge-eating.

E   The binge-eating is not associated with the regular use of inappropriate compensatory behaviors (e.g., purging, fasting, excessive exercise) and does not occur exclusively during the course of anorexia
nervosa or bulimia nervosa.

# Postscript to Part One

Part One of this book has set out to provide a brief account of the nature of binge-eating and bulimia nervosa. If you have read thus far because you have problems with your eating, it should now be clear to you whether or not you have bulimia nervosa or some variation of this disorder. Similarly, if you have a friend or relative with bulimia nervosa, you should by now have an idea of the sorts of problems they experience with eating, and the kinds of effects these problems will be having on their life.

If you have problems controlling your eating, the question will now arise: What should you do about it? Chapter 5 has briefly outlined the sorts of treatment available for bulimia nervosa. You may conclude that your problems are not sufficiently serious to merit special attention and you may be happy to ignore them. Or you may recognize yourself in the descriptions given of people with bulimia nervosa and appreciate, if you have not done so already, that you need help. In this case you should certainly read Part Two of this book. This is a self-help manual for people with bulimia nervosa and variations of this disorder, and offers a practical guide to recovery. It has already been used by a great number of people with bulimia nervosa, to their considerable benefit.

If you have read Part One of this book because of concern for a friend or relative who has bulimia nervosa or a related binge-eating problem, you could also benefit from reading Part Two. It will help you to appreciate the considerable efforts which someone who binges has to make in order to recover. It will also help you to assist, rather than unwittingly to hinder, the progress of someone with the disorder who is attempting to use this book as a route to recovery.

PART TWO

# A Self-Help Manual

*for People with Binge-Eating
Problems and Bulimia Nervosa*

# Introduction

Many people who have problems controlling their eating manage to overcome their difficulties without seeking professional help. Some will have run into difficulties relatively recently and their disturbed eating will not therefore have become a habit. Others will have had problems for many years but never seriously got around to trying to do something about putting things right. For some the process of restoring their eating habits to normal is a relatively simple matter of starting to eat sensibly again. For many others the task is a very difficult one, yet somehow they do succeed. They manage to stop binge-eating. They stop making themselves sick. They stop taking laxatives. They eat ordinary meals at regular times. And, most important of all, food and eating cease to dominate their lives and they stop being so intensely concerned about their weight and their shape. In other words, they start to lead 'normal' lives again.

Sadly, many other people with very similar problems turn up in specialist clinics having been unable, after repeated efforts, to manage on their own. It is not necessarily that their problems have been around longer or that their eating habits are more severely disturbed. It is just that the things they tried to do to improve matters simply did not work. And often they made things considerably worse. Now, of course, many people with bulimia nervosa will need specialist help and it is important that they seek such help and receive it. But many others could, if they knew how to go about it, manage to restore their eating habits to normal on their own. This self-help manual is intended to provide guidelines for people who want to try to manage on their own but are unsure where to begin.

## For Whom is this Manual Intended?

The guidelines that follow are aimed at people who have what might be termed 'classic bulimia nervosa': that is to say, people who regularly lose control of their eating and binge, attempt to compensate for the episodes of overeating in extreme ways (e.g. by fasting, vomiting or taking laxatives), and who regard their body shape or weight as of great personal significance, to the extent that concerns about weight and shape dominate their lives.

Of course, there are many other people who do not quite fit this description but who share some of the same features. They may binge very occasionally. They may not binge but regularly make themselves sick after meals or after eating any food they believe to be potentially fattening. They may alternate between periods of relatively normal eating and days of strict fasting to lose weight. They may regularly take laxatives to compensate for eating what they regard as fattening food. The guidelines that follow are also likely to be of use to these people. Although some of what is discussed may not be relevant to them, the general principles apply to all people who are experiencing difficulty controlling their eating and want to restore their disturbed eating habits to normal and to put their concerns about their weight and shape into a manageable perspective.

Some people who binge but do not have bulimia nervosa may find that some of this manual does not apply to them. For them the manual in *Overcoming Binge Eating* by Christopher Fairburn is likely to be more appropriate.

## For Whom is this Manual not Appropriate?

There are six categories of people with bulimia nervosa for whom this manual is probably not appropriate.

(1) For some people who are rigidly locked into a pattern of grossly disturbed eating habits, the idea of their being able

to break out of the cycle on their own may not be realistic. It is important to add here that many people who do not belong to this category will think that they do. If you are prepared to *try* to change some aspects of your current eating habits, then you almost certainly do not belong to this category.

(2) Some people who are completely socially isolated may well need the support and encouragement of a therapist they can see regularly.

(3) Some people who are so demoralized and disheartened that they cannot muster up the energy to begin to try to change will probably not be able to make use of this manual.

(4) For some people whose body weight is very low (and, in addition to bulimia nervosa, are suffering from anorexia nervosa), it is possible that the guidelines contained in this manual could actually do them harm rather than improve matters.

(5) For some people the eating disorder is only one relatively minor feature of much wider difficulties, such as problems with alcohol, self-harm (such as cutting themselves or repeatedly taking overdoses) and their relationships; they will need more help than that provided in this manual.

(6) People with a medical condition in which eating can have a significant impact (such as diabetes), and women who are pregnant, need to place themselves in medical care.

If you belong to one or more of these six categories you will need specialist help and you should consult your doctor about being referred for treatment. For all of these groups specific treatments are available, and the prospects of being helped are good if such treatment is received.

In fact, this manual is likely to be of help to the great majority of those with bulimia nervosa and related problems. This statement can be made with confidence because the effectiveness of the manual has been studied. More than eighty people with bulimia nervosa who were referred by their doctor were given the manual. They used it for four to six months and were then re-evaluated. The great majority of them had improved substantially and regarded themselves as no longer in need of help. Some of these people have written accounts of their use of the manual, four of which have been included at the end of this book (Appendix 3).


## Some Points to Consider Before You Start

*Making Change a High Priority*
Overcoming difficulties with eating is seldom easy and is usually very hard indeed. It is therefore essential, if you are to make a serious effort at doing so, to make this task a very high priority in your life. *Restoring your eating habits to normal must be your first priority*; and other responsibilities will have to fall in line behind this priority. This may sound like awful advice. You may well feel that it is totally against your principles to act so 'selfishly'. But it is really the responsible thing to do because it is only by overcoming your eating problems that you can properly take on your wider personal and social commitments. So, if you feel reluctant to give your own problems such a high priority at the expense of the needs of others, you can reassure yourself that it would really be in everyone else's best interests if you did so.

*Why is it Worth Changing?*
While it is true that it is difficult to overcome bulimia nervosa, doing so is immensely worthwhile. To most people this conclusion is so obvious that it is hardly worth stating. But some people might need a certain amount of convincing. There are three main reasons why restoring eating habits to normal is worth the effort involved.

*Psychological reasons*   There are a number of psychological consequences of bulimia nervosa and related disturbances in eating habits which make overcoming these problems worthwhile. Considerable shame and guilt frequently surround binge-eating and vomiting. This leads people to live a secret and lonely existence, sometimes for many years, and makes them feel inferior to others – even, at times, quite worthless. Also, severe

60

depression commonly sets in after a binge, and this can last for some time. Some people undergo wild mood swings, usually in response to their degree of control over their eating, such that they change rapidly from feeling extremely happy to feeling utterly miserable. Often people feel very anxious in situations involving exposure to food, such as eating out, eating in front of others, or preparing food for other people. The constant preoccupation with weight, shape, food and eating often makes concentrating difficult. Indeed, it is common for people to feel that their lives are totally dominated by thoughts about food and eating and concerns about weight and shape. Reinstating 'normal' eating habits reverses many of these difficulties and is a major step towards resolving the others.

*Social reasons*   Bulimia nervosa takes a great toll in terms of one's social life. Personal relationships are badly affected. At worst, binge-eating and vomiting occur many times a day and there is simply no time to lead anything approximating a normal life. The truth is that much of social life involves eating with other people. Many people with bulimia nervosa solve this particular problem by always eating on their own. Also, it is common for people to feel fat and unattractive after a binge and not to want to be seen by anyone. So they avoid company and again choose to remain on their own. Unfortunately, under these circumstances they are much more likely to binge. Family relationships frequently become strained.

In addition, for a number of reasons work can be adversely affected. Food-related situations are particularly problematic. For example, there can be major difficulties in dealing with the cafeteria or coffee breaks. Also, as noted above, thoughts of food and eating and concerns about weight and shape can interfere with the ability to concentrate to such an extent that performance at work can suffer. People find it difficult to keep track of what they are doing; and they find it impossible to focus on a particular task, ending up, for example, reading something over and over again, quite unable to take anything in.

Even if one is apparently coping quite well, the feelings of depression and worthlessness which the binge-eating and vomiting cause can make one feel generally inadequate and unconfident at work and socially. Again, all these difficulties improve considerably when one's eating habits return to normal.

*Medical reasons* There are a number of potential medical complications associated with bulimia nervosa and binge-eating. Some of these arise as a result of the binge-eating and others as a result of the methods to which people resort to compensate for overeating (vomiting, taking laxatives, and so on). Some of these complications are common, such as abdominal pain, salivary gland swelling and sore throats. Rarely, there can be more serious complications, such as damage to the stomach wall or the esophagus. Repeated vomiting and frequent laxative-taking can disturb the body's fluid balance and lead to hypo-kalemia (low potassium), which can cause irregularities in heartbeat.

All of these potential physical hazards add force to the argument that it is worth making an effort to recover. It is important to emphasize that the majority of these physical complications are reversible. That is, when normal eating habits are re-established, the body readjusts and returns to a healthy state.

The disturbed eating habits of people who binge can complicate the course of pregnancy. If you are pregnant and binge-eating, or dieting or vomiting or taking laxatives, diuretics or other pills, you should discuss these matters frankly with your doctor.

These are some of the reasons why it is worthwhile committing yourself to overcoming your eating difficulties. No doubt there are other, perhaps more compelling, personal reasons for doing so. Whatever your particular reasons for wishing to change, it is important to emphasize at the outset that *you will not be able to stop binge-eating and resume 'normal' eating unless you are very highly motivated to do so.* By the same token, if you really want to change and are prepared to make a major commitment to doing so, there is every reason to expect that you will be successful.

*Is Now the Right Time to Tackle Your Eating Problems?*
It is worth considering, before going any further with this manual, whether now is the right time for you to be tackling this problem. If you are about to go on holiday in two weeks, or you are studying for exams, you will not be able to devote yourself properly to the principles outlined below. In such circumstances, it would be best if you postponed beginning the program until the time is right and you can make the necessary commitment. If you make a half-hearted start and then run into difficulties you may well become disheartened and give up on something that might work for you under the right circumstances. On the other hand, unless there is a serious reason for not starting with this program now, like the two examples given above, you should commit yourself to beginning at a definite time in the near future. There will always be sufficient trivial reasons for postponing beginning this program and you should be suspicious of weak excuses.

## 'Why Can't I Just Stop Binge-Eating?'

Before setting out the program you should follow in tackling your difficulties with eating, it is worth describing the kinds of factors operating to prevent people with bulimia nervosa from just getting better spontaneously. It may seem odd that bulimia nervosa continues when the behavior in which people engage is so contrary to how they want to behave and when it makes them

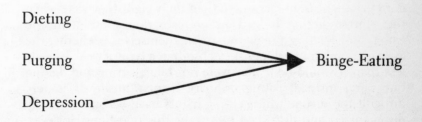

Figure 1   The three main factors that perpetuate binge-eating

so miserable. The reason for this is that people unwittingly adopt methods of coping which are counter-productive. For example, fasting after a binge may make you feel better temporarily, but it also significantly increases the chances that you will binge again. The three main factors which serve to perpetuate bulimia nervosa are shown in figure 1.

*Dieting*
Most young women at some time go on a diet to lose weight. However, it is a sad fact that, despite the effort and commitment and the money invested in diet literature and diet regimes, these attempts are rarely successful. Moreover, there is good evidence that dieting places people under physiological and psychological pressures to eat and, paradoxically, causes overeating. For the great majority of people with bulimia nervosa, binge-eating began after they had started dieting. And for all of them, it is dieting that keeps the binge-eating going. In order to over-come bulimia nervosa and be confident of being able to eat 'normally' *you are going to have to give up the idea of dieting.* Of course, this is a terrible prospect for someone who has dieted for years and who is terrified that to stop doing so would inevitably lead to her becoming fat. But, for anyone reading this guide in the hope that it might contain information which will help you deal with your eating problems, it is a simple truth that dieting has not worked: you are almost certainly heavier than you want to be and, despite wanting to lose weight, you periodically lose control and binge, which is guaranteed to prevent you from losing weight. It is also the case that for most people their current weight is, in fact, more than the weight they were when they started dieting. Indeed, an interesting question for anyone who is binge-eating and dieting to ask themselves is whether the average number of calories they absorb in a typical week is really less than it would be if they were not binge-eating and dieting but were, instead, eating ordinary regular meals. It is very difficult for anyone whose eating habits have become seriously disorganized and disturbed to answer this question. However, the truth is that, whatever efforts one goes to in order to compensate for overeating, a large number of calories is absorbed

from a binge; and, in fact, *it is usual that people who replace a pattern of dieting and binge-eating with regular meals do not gain weight.* Some people actually lose weight. It is very rare that normal eating leads to significant weight gain.

Having read the previous section, you may well be thinking: 'Well, if I am not allowed to diet, this program is not for me.' This is an understandable response; but it must be repeated in the strongest terms that *dieting has not worked for you and it is a major factor causing you to binge.* You may well reply that, while it is true that dieting has failed in the sense that your eating habits are disorganized and out of control, it is, nevertheless, the case that if you were not dieting you would be even worse off since you would be eating far too much and would be gaining weight and in no time would be fat. This is a very strong conviction and a very compelling fear for many people with bulimia nervosa. However, it is a conviction which is almost certainly wrong and a fear which is almost certainly unfounded. *The truth is that for most people the replacement of a pattern of dieting and binge-eating with 'normal' meals does not have a significant effect on their weight.* It will be very difficult for anyone who has these convictions and fears to accept this rebuttal on faith. The only way forward is to try the following experiment: for a four-week trial period commit yourself to sticking to all the principles spelled out in this manual and, after the four weeks, assess whether there has been an improvement in your eating habits and see what has happened to your weight. The answers to these questions will help you decide whether it is worth continuing with the program.

*Purging (Vomiting and Taking Laxatives)*
Vomiting encourages overeating. It is very common for people to say that when they first discovered vomiting as a method of dealing with overeating they felt elated. Suddenly they could eat what they wanted without it affecting their weight. However, they soon discovered that, far from liberating them, *vomiting is a trap: vomiting leads to more eating which in turn leads to more vomiting.* And a vicious cycle is established where vomiting comes, in part, to encourage binge-eating. Indeed, many people

with bulimia nervosa find that, if they know that the circumstances are such that they are not going to be able to vomit (for example, if they are going on a long car journey with friends), this acts as a temporary brake on their eating. The implication for someone who wants to restore their eating habits to normal is that by stopping vomiting they will be encouraged to exert more control over their eating. It is, of course, not as simple as this and giving up vomiting as a method of escaping the consequences of overeating is far from easy. To some extent the same argument applies to the use of laxatives (see the section below headed 'Some Advice').

*Depression*
Depression often causes people with bulimia nervosa to binge. And binges make people depressed. Thus, another vicious cycle is set up. Now, if you are making an effort not to binge then you will be attempting to break out of this cycle. However, many things other than overeating can make you feel depressed and thereby indirectly lead you to binge. The implication here is that it is important for you to examine which aspects of your life are unsatisfactory and cause you to feel depressed, and to attempt to find solutions to these difficulties (see the advice about problem solving in Step 4 below).

*Other Factors that may Perpetuate Binge-Eating*
There are a number of other factors which serve to perpetuate binge-eating. *One important factor is a very low body weight.* This is not usually a problem in bulimia nervosa because most people with the disorder are within the 'normal' weight range. But for some people whose body weight is very low, the body is, in effect, in a state of starvation and this in itself seems to cause binge-eating. For people in this situation binge-eating cannot be overcome completely unless they allow their body weight to rise to a healthy level (see below under 'Some Advice').

There are other factors, too, which can make it more likely that a binge will take place (such as drinking alcohol), and it is important that these are identified and steps taken to eliminate their effect (see Step 3, 'Learning to Intervene').

## Do You Require Help in Addition to that Provided in this Manual?

The guidelines spelled out below are essentially practical. They arise from an acceptance of the problems with eating at face value: that is, that there are people who are distressed by being unable to control their eating and who want help in restoring their eating habits to normal. The manual is intended to provide these people with the tools they need to recover. The guidelines are not, therefore, intended to help you uncover any deep reasons which might have caused your eating to become disordered in the first place. The reason for this is simply that the process of uncovering hidden causes is not necessary for restoring eating habits to 'normal'. That is to say, *it is perfectly possible for someone with bulimia nervosa to overcome her problems with eating simply by focusing on changing her eating habits and her attitudes towards weight and shape.* Given that this is possible, it seems sensible to specify how someone might achieve this end on her own.

Of course, some people may feel that the problems they have, including their eating disorder, arise directly from aspects of their early experience of which they want a deeper understanding, and they may well feel that a course of psychotherapy would be helpful to them in this regard. Similarly, some people may feel that a course of counselling would help them to deal with the day-to-day stresses of their lives. Following the guidelines set out in this manual is not at odds with either of these options. Psychotherapy and counselling do not stand in opposition to your dealing with your eating problems yourself; and you may feel that they would actually help you manage better with the manual. However, it must be emphasized that while they may or may not be helpful to you, it is usually perfectly reasonable to expect that you will be able to restore order to your eating habits without such additional help.

## About the Self-Help Program

This self-help program is not intended to be a comprehensive record of everything one could imagine doing that might be helpful in restoring eating habits to normal. It would be a formidable task to produce such a record because it would need to include so many variations applicable to such a wide range of people. It would also be confusing to find one's way around and probably would not be very helpful to many people. Instead, the manual provided here consists of the *basic elements* of a self-help program. Much of the specific detail will need to be filled in by you and will depend on your particular circumstances and what sort of person you are. The manual is intended to be what might be termed a *basic treatment*: that is, it consists of the minimum requirements necessary for restoring eating habits to 'normal'. This minimal treatment is set out on the assumption that it will be sufficiently helpful to many people with bulimia nervosa to enable them to deal with their eating problems without specialist help. It is, however, important to state again that for some people it may not be sufficient and it is important that they consult their doctor about finding additional help.

The treatment program described below is highly structured. It assumes that you want to overcome your eating difficulties and that you want advice on how to go about doing so. This advice is given. It is, of course, entirely up to you which pieces of advice you choose to accept and which you do not. However, all the components of the program are known to be helpful to patients with bulimia nervosa receiving treatment in specialist clinics, and the more of the advice you choose not to follow the less likely it is that the program will be helpful to you in restoring control to your eating. Conversely, *the extent to which this manual is going to be useful to you depends on how strictly you can adhere to its guidelines*. In some sense, if this manual is going to help you, it is necessary for you to trust it all more or less as an act of faith. However, given that you have read this far and it is therefore likely that you do not know how to proceed with helping yourself, it is an act of faith probably worth making, at least on a trial basis.

# Introduction

The self-help program spelled out below places considerable demands on you. As you read on you may well feel overwhelmed by how much you are going to have to do to overcome your problems with eating. Do not be too daunted. First, the program builds up slowly, in steps, and you can set the pace. Second, although the program specifies definite steps you must take in order to recover, *it is not intended that you should follow these steps for ever*. Indeed, the goal of this treatment is that you should be able to reach a position where food is no longer a threat to you, where you can eat normally and with enjoyment and without anxieties about your weight and shape. To arrive at such a goal, however, it is necessary to proceed via a route that does involve thinking a great deal about food and eating and about your weight and shape. In other words, in order to free yourself of your anxieties, for a period of time it will be necessary for you to pay particular attention to your eating and your concerns about weight and shape. How long it will take to recover varies greatly from individual to individual. Most people with bulimia nervosa who can make use of this manual work through it in about six months. Some manage to do it in a shorter period and some need longer. It would be a mistake to concern yourself at this stage with how long it will take for you. However, if you find that you have made a real effort to use the manual and have not been able to make any progress at all in, say, around six weeks, then it would be sensible to stop trying to use it alone and consult your doctor about getting further help. If, on the other hand, you have made even just a little progress, over some months, then as long as you continue to progress it is worth persevering.

## The Six Steps
There are six steps to the self-help program. These are listed in figure 2 (p. 71), and these six steps follow each other in the order given: having established regular monitoring of your eating (Step 1), you move on to setting up a meal plan (Step 2) while continuing with the monitoring; and, having set up a meal plan, you move on to learning to intervene in times of difficulty (Step 3), in the context of your meal plan

69

(while continuing to monitor your eating); and so on. At the end of each step there is a 'Review Box'. This consists of a set of questions, which you should ask yourself, concerning the progress you have made. Only when you are able to answer 'yes' to all the questions should you proceed to the next step in the manual.

## How to Use this Manual

This manual contains a lot of information. If you read right through it, put it aside, and then attempt to follow all the advice at once, you will not succeed. It is essential that you follow the steps in the order they come and only go on to the next step when you are ready to do so. It is a good idea to read through the entire manual first to get an overall idea of the sort of information it contains. For some people who have serious difficulties in concentrating, the prospect of reading through the entire manual will be too daunting. What they should do is spend just ten minutes skimming through the manual, perhaps just reading the headings and subheadings; this will be sufficient for them to get a rough idea of what the manual contains. Having read through the manual (or skimmed through it), you will be ready to begin Step 1. However, you will not be able to remember in sufficient detail from one reading what is contained in Step 1, so you will have to re-read it. In fact, you will need to refer to the manual again and again and it would therefore be sensible for you to carry it around with you. It might help you to mark the sections that are especially relevant to where you are in the program. In addition, if you attempt to follow some particular piece of advice given in the manual and it does not work out as planned, you should go back to the relevant section, re-read it, and try to determine why things went wrong and what you should do next time to improve your chances of succeeding.

### *Recruiting a Helper or Advocate*
Some people whose eating is not very seriously disturbed will be able to make use of this manual entirely on their own. However,

## Introduction

### Step 1. Monitoring

**(keeping a systematic written record of your eating so that you can know precisely what has been happening)**

↓

### Step 2. Establishing a meal plan

**(deciding on what pattern of eating is sensible and attempting to adhere to it)**

↓

### Step 3. Learning to intervene

**(learning what sort of circumstances cause you to binge and what sort of things you can do to prevent this happening)**

↓

### Step 4. Problem solving

**(learning how to define problems which cause you difficulty with your eating and learning to deal with them)**

↓

### Step 5. Eliminating dieting

**(systematically widening the range of foods you eat)**

↓

### Step 6. Changing your mind

**(identifying some of the beliefs which underlie your difficulties with eating and attempting to modify them)**

Figure 2   An outline of the self-help program presented in this manual

for many people with bulimia nervosa this is an unrealistic expectation. The problem is that, however hard you try to stick to the guidelines set out in the treatment program, there will inevitably be times when things do not go well. At these times it is difficult not to become depressed, to blame yourself and to feel like giving up. Having someone to talk to at these times, to go over what has happened and what you might be able to do about it, can be invaluable. Such a person could be a close friend or relative. However, it is usually better for such a helper to be someone with whom you do not have a close relationship in your ordinary life; someone who is less intimately involved with you and who can therefore be objective. Your doctor or the health-care provider (in the UK, the practice nurse) is probably a better person to choose than a friend. It is particularly good if you can see your helper regularly. Ideally this should be every week at first, but it soon can be less frequent than this.

At the end of this manual there is a brief section for helpers or advocates (Appendix 2). You should show this to the person you ask to help you.

*Keeping Going: Be Prepared for a Struggle*
It is common for people, having read right through the manual, to feel charged up with enthusiasm to tackle their difficulties with eating. It is also common for people to feel, the first time that something goes wrong, that they have totally failed and will never succeed. It is important to stress that *if overcoming your problems with eating were easy, you would have done so long ago*. It is going to be a struggle and there will be times when you will not manage to achieve as much as you want to. However, if you are attempting to follow the guidelines set out in this manual, you are making an effort at taking control of your eating; and *any success at all is an improvement on which further improvements can be built*. Do not imagine that you can follow all the manual's principles tomorrow and that you will therefore never binge again. Replacing disorganized eating habits with a 'normal' pattern of eating is usually a slow and painful process in which there are a great many attempts which fail. However, if you do try to follow the principles set out here and make rational decisions about how to proceed, you will almost certainly make progress. And if you are making progress, however slowly, it is worth persevering. Many people find that at some point, perhaps some months after starting out, suddenly things become much easier and the prospect of a life of 'normal' eating becomes a possibility they can genuinely imagine. So if you are just creeping forward, it is well worth carrying on and waiting for the breakthrough.

# Introduction

## Some Advice about Weight and Weight Control

Before describing the six steps in the self-help program, it is important that you are armed with certain information which will be of help to you. In particular, it would be useful to reconsider what is an appropriate weight for you; it would be helpful to establish a regular system of weighing yourself; and it is worth considering how effective vomiting and purgative use actually are at getting rid of unwanted calories.

### How Much Should You Weigh?

It is very difficult for anyone to pronounce on what is the 'correct' weight for you. Some people argue that your weight should not be allowed to fall more than 15 per cent below the average for your age, height and sex. The basis for this argument is that below such a weight the physiological and psychological effects of starvation will make it virtually impossible for you to eat normally. Others argue that the 'correct' weight is the weight you were before your problems with eating began. Both of these definitions can be helpful in many cases, but neither is entirely satisfactory. Some people whose relatives are all overweight, and whose natural weight is higher than the average, would experience starvation symptoms well before they weighed 15 per cent less than the average. And for many people with bulimia nervosa who have a long history of disturbed eating habits of one sort or another, it is impossible to identify a point at which their eating was sufficiently 'normal' to identify a natural body weight.

The range of appropriate weights is shown in figure 3. You might find it helpful to consider what would be a healthy weight for a person of your height. It may also be worth your considering where the weight you would ideally like to be is in relation to the norms shown in the figure. Many people with bulimia nervosa want to be at a very low weight, and if they are going to recover from their eating disorder and manage to eat normally they are going to have to give up this desire to weigh so little and replace it with a more realistic target weight range.

Natural weight will vary considerably from one individual to another. 'Natural weight' means the weight at which your body would settle if you were eating perfectly normally. This weight is determined by two things: first, genetic factors (i.e. factors which you have inherited from your parents), which have a strong influence on your natural weight; and second, the balance between how much you eat and the energy you expend. Now, it is most unlikely that you will have an accurate idea of what

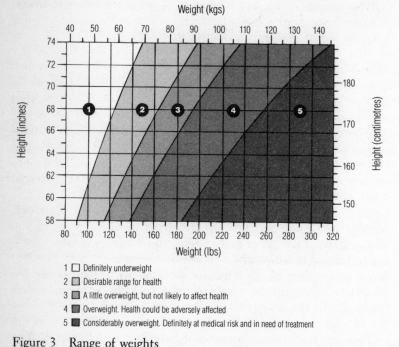

1 ☐ Definitely underweight
2 ▨ Desirable range for health
3 ▨ A little overweight, but not likely to affect health
4 ▨ Overweight. Health could be adversely affected
5 ■ Considerably overweight. Definitely at medical risk and in need of treatment

Figure 3   Range of weights
*Source*:   Adapted from *Obesity and Related Diseases* by John Garrow (1988), by kind permission of Churchill Livingstone.

this weight would be if you were eating normally; and it is very likely that, if you were to make a guess, you would substantially overestimate the true figure. The truth is that *the only way to discover what your natural weight is, is to reinstate normal eating habits and then see over a period of several months what happens to your weight*. It is also important to remember that weight does not ordinarily sit at one fixed point. Rather, it is quite 'normal' for body weight to fluctuate within the space of a week by a few pounds in both directions. So if you do have in your mind an acceptable weight this should be a range of acceptability (with a two- or three-pound margin in either direction) rather than one fixed number. You must also remember that weight changes occur naturally over the menstrual cycle. Premenstrual water retention, bloatedness and 'weight gain' are very common and a result of normal hormonal changes.

As noted above, it is usual for the weight of people who follow the principles set out ,in this self-help guide not to change significantly. Some people do lose weight. However, most people never achieve the weight they would ideally like to be. This is because their ideal weight is usually unrealistically low and simply not achievable without starving themselves to a point where they would be at serious medical risk. It has to be added here that the vast majority of women with no particular eating problem also want to weigh much less than they do; and they also almost always fail to achieve this low weight. However, the important point here for people with bulimia nervosa is that there is often a trade-off to be made between weight and eating habits: thus, you may well find that, having stuck to this self-help program, you will be able to eat normally but that your weight is, say, a few pounds more than you would like it to be. But, if you diet and lose those few pounds, then you will not be able to maintain control of your eating and binge-eating will return. Ultimately the choice here will be entirely yours. The question is: '*Is weighing a few pounds more than you are entirely happy with a worthwhile price to pay for normal eating habits and the kind of life that this permits?*' Or, to put it the other way round: '*Is weighing a few pounds less a worthwhile goal given that the cost is perpetually disturbed eating habits and the effect they have on the rest of your life?*'

If you follow this treatment program it is likely that you will eventually be faced with the questions posed above. It is not worth considering your answer in any detail at this point because you do not know the exact nature of the choice; nor will you know until you are eating normally and your weight has settled at some point. Some people are very lucky and their weight settles at exactly the point they always wished it to be. Others are less fortunate. For the great majority the outcome is the same as it is for everybody else: their weight is a little above what they would prefer it to be. *The sensible thing to do at this stage, when you are just beginning to try to restore some order to your eating habits, is to postpone any decision about your weight and about what weight would be acceptable to you until you have regained control of your eating and seen precisely what effect this has actually had on your weight.*

## Weighing Yourself

There are two common ways in which people with bulimia nervosa deal with weighing themselves. Some get on and off the scales frequently, to check what effect binge-eating, vomiting, and so on has had on their weight. Many others avoid weighing themselves altogether because the effect of doing so is too distressing. Many alternate between the two extremes, depending on the degree of control over their eating and whether their weight is high or low. Neither solution is satisfactory. Frequent weighing merely serves to increase the level of concern and preoccupation with weight by highlighting small and insignificant fluctuations; and completely avoiding weighing also increases anxiety about what the weight might really be. Certainly, establishing a meal plan and attempting to follow it, as you will do if you follow the manual, does have direct implications for your weight, and if you are to make rational decisions about your behavior you ought to be aware of exactly what these implications are. *The appropriate solution is to weigh yourself once a week.* This should be at the same time each week (Friday morning is a good time for many people) and, given that on some occasions this may be an upsetting experience for you (and when you are upset you are likely to feel like eating), it is wise to choose a time of the day when it is going to be difficult for you to eat (such as just before you have to leave the house for work). You should record your weight so you can track its progress. Weighing should be obligatory. *You should not weigh yourself at any time other than your set weekly time.*

For some people this is going to be a very difficult task. If you have avoided weighing yourself for some time you will find it difficult to begin. Unfortunately there is no easy way to start: you will simply have to steel yourself. But you can be reassured that once you have started it can become a relatively simple routine. On the other hand, if you are weighing yourself frequently, say, many times a day, it will be very difficult to restrict weighing to once a week. In such circumstances you should put yourself on a program to cut down the frequency of weighing. For example, for the first week you should restrict weighing to once a day. For the second week you should weigh every second day. And so on. *By the end of four weeks you should be on the once a week weighing schedule.*

*Checking Body Shape*
It is common for people with bulimia nervosa to make frequent checks on their body shape, just as they might make frequent checks on their weight. So they might use a tape measure to judge the 'fatness' of particular parts of their body, such as their thighs or their waist. They might make regular inspections of themselves in the mirror. And they might pinch certain parts of themselves (like their stomach) to gauge how 'fat' they are. *Checking your body shape in this way is not a good idea and you should try to stop doing it.* Making these sorts of checks simply serves to increase your concerns about your shape. You feel happy when the check produces a desirable result and distressed when the results are unsatisfactory. And the problem is that these responses then come to govern your subsequent actions. Thus, it is common for people who have examined themselves in the mirror and decided that they are fat to immediately go and binge. It is important, therefore, that you stop making such checks of your body shape. If necessary, you can phase out these checks gradually, as described above for people who weigh themselves very often. However, the sooner they are stopped the better.

Some people judge their body shape by how tight their clothes feel. This too serves to maintain the preoccupation with shape and size. It is, incidentally, quite an unreliable method because some clothes shrink when they are washed; and the result is that one feels fatter when one is wearing clean clothes. If you habitually judge your shape by the feel of your clothes, then it would be well worth your while taking all your clothes which are tight (jeans and skirts are especially important) and either altering them so that they fit more loosely or getting rid of them. Some people keep in the wardrobe clothes they used to wear some time ago when they were much thinner. Their intention is to start wearing them again when they have successfully reduced their weight. *This is a most unhelpful practice*. It encourages dieting which, in turn, encourages binge-eating. And the small clothes are a depressing reminder that you are not as thin as you would like to be. It would be best if you got rid of these clothes.

*Vomiting*
Clearly an important aspect of restoring your eating habits to normal is for you to stop vomiting. For most people this will follow naturally once they have established a pattern of regular eating and have stopped the binges. Some people, however, will need to make a special effort. It is important to remember that vomiting encourages overeating. So, in a sense, *the more you vomit the more you will overeat*. A basic principle you should try to follow is that you should *always try not to eat anything that you know you will feel unable to keep down* (see Step 2, 'Instituting a Meal Plan').

A fact that comes as something of a surprise to most people with bulimia nervosa is that *vomiting does not really work*. Its purpose is to get rid of the food eaten, usually in a binge, so that the calories ingested will not be absorbed. The reason this purpose is not achieved by vomiting is that binges usually involve the consumption of a large number of calories and vomiting does not retrieve all of them. In fact, a significant proportion of the calories consumed in a binge will be absorbed by the stomach and small intestine. What this means is that usually *the number of calories absorbed from binges, even after vomiting, is greater than the number that would have been absorbed in a binge-free day during which normal meals and snacks had been eaten*.

*Laxative Misuse*

Some people who find it difficult to make themselves sick take laxatives as an alternative method of compensating for binge-eating. Others who do vomit after binges take laxatives as a further 'guarantee' that calories are not absorbed. *Laxatives are wholly ineffective as a method of losing weight or compensating for overeating.* They have a minimal effect on the absorption of calories, and the small influence they do have on body weight is achieved by changing the body's fluid balance (essentially, through water lost in diarrhea). This is a temporary effect because one inevitably gets thirsty and drinks, and the restoration of the lost fluids reverses the apparent weight loss. Even if you have felt that some physical cost to taking purgatives would be worth it for the benefit to your weight, given that there is no such benefit *there really is no point at all in continuing taking laxatives.*

There are many problems associated with the use of laxatives. One is that the body develops tolerance to them, and people find that in order to experience the laxative effect, they have to increase the dose steadily. One consequence of this is that when they try to stop taking the laxatives, or try to cut down the number they take, they become constipated. Another problem is that the body retains water in an attempt to compensate for the laxative effect, leading to puffiness and swelling. If you are taking only small amounts of laxatives occasionally there should be no difficulty in your stopping this immediately. If you take them regularly it may be helpful for you to phase them out gradually. Certainly, if you take a large quantity, a phasing-out process is advisable to avoid the 'withdrawal' effects described above. You may also benefit from taking one of the commercially available fiber supplements (in the normal prescribed dose) to counteract any constipation. If you are regularly taking large quantities of laxatives and cannot manage to phase them out even with the help of a fiber supplement, you should consult your doctor for help.

Some people say that even though they know that laxatives are no help to them in controlling their weight or in compensating for overeating, they serve another purpose which makes them want to continue taking them. One such purpose is to make them 'feel empty', which is a comfort, particularly after a binge. Another reason people give for taking laxatives is that their effect is exceedingly unpleasant and they are used as a form of self-punishment. Neither of these 'purposes' is helpful and they must be put aside. If you are working at a program for restoring your eating habits to normal you must do only what is good for you and what will help you, and *you should reward yourself for doing well, not punish yourself for lapses*.

## Diuretic Misuse
Diuretics, which are pills designed to reduce the body's water content by encouraging urination, have no real effect on body weight; as with laxative use, any appearance to the contrary is the result solely of temporary effects on fluid balance. They are of no benefit to you at all and you should not take them (unless, of course, they have been prescribed by a doctor for a medical reason).

## Excessive Exercise
Exercise is much encouraged these days because of its positive benefits to health; and many people with bulimia nervosa say that they definitely feel much better about themselves when they are taking regular exercise. However, it is also the case that many people use excessive exercise as a method of compensating for overeating. This is not healthy and serves to perpetuate concerns about food, eating, weight and shape. If you are using exercise primarily as a means of weight control, you should keep a record of exactly how much time you are spending exercising. This can then be reviewed and you can institute a program of appropriate exercise. You may well find this difficult and it may be necessary for you to reduce the amount you exercise in stages. The aim is for you to exercise because you enjoy it and because it is physically good for you. *Any exercise which is taken principally for weight control reasons or to compensate for overeating is not advisable*.

## 'Diet Pills'
Drugs which suppress your appetite (like amphetamines) do have a temporary effect on eating. However, they also have a

number of physical and psychological side-effects. They are also addictive. It is most inadvisable to take them to help you to avoid eating. They should never be taken unless under medical supervision. Most importantly, when people stop taking them their eating returns to just the same state as it was in before they took them.

# Step 1

# *Monitoring Your Eating*

*Note: Read through all of Step 1 before beginning to try to implement the principles outlined in this section.*

## The Purpose of Monitoring

If you are going to begin trying to change your eating habits then it is important that you know exactly what is happening with your eating at the moment. For this reason *it is essential that you keep a detailed record every day of when you eat, what you eat, where you eat, whether you felt that what you ate was excessive, whether you felt out of control, whether you vomited or took laxatives, and other circumstances that might be relevant to reorganizing your eating habits*. At first keeping such a record might seem both tedious and pointless. It might even seem like a punishment, in that by making you more aware of your eating habits it makes you feel worse. However, for you to begin to change it is necessary that you do become aware of exactly what is happening with your eating; and it will soon become apparent that this record is an invaluable aid in this process.

## General Guidelines for Monitoring

In keeping this record, it will be helpful for you to stick to the following guidelines:

(1) Use a standard form (see below for example).
(2) Use a separate sheet (or sheets if necessary) for each day.

83

(3) Record everything you eat (not just things you feel happy about having eaten), and do not abandon monitoring when your eating goes wrong.

(4) Write down what you have eaten immediately after having done so, rather than trying to remember everything at the end of the day.

### Specific Guidelines for Monitoring

An example of one person's monitoring sheet for one day is shown in figure 4.

(1) The first column is for recording the time when food is eaten. Try to be reasonably accurate about this because, as will emerge later, it is important.

(2) The second column is for recording all the food (and liquid) that you consume during the day. As already noted, it is important to write this down soon after the episode of eating. To do this it is obviously necessary that you carry the monitoring sheet or notebook with you at all times. When writing down the food you should be reasonably precise about what you have eaten. So if you eat two chocolate bars, rather than just writing down 'chocolate', you should record it as, say, 'two Mars bars'. However, you should not be so precise as to weigh food and record the weights (like '100 grams All Bran', when 'a small bowl of All Bran' would do); and *you should not record the calorie content*. A simple description of what you ate is perfectly adequate. Since the aim of your following this self-help program is to restore healthy eating habits, it is important that you indicate on your monitoring sheets when you ate a normal meal. It may be difficult for you to decide on what is and what is not a 'normal meal'. What is meant is an episode of eating where food is eaten in a controlled and organized manner. The amount eaten should not influence your decision here. As long as you intended to eat certain food, and did so without feeling out of control and in a normal fashion, then this can be regarded as a meal. These

| Time | Food and liquid consumed | Place | B | C | Context of overeating/vomiting |
|---|---|---|---|---|---|
| 7.30 | Black Coffee × 2 | Kitchen | | | Weight: 8st 3lbs. Weight up 3lbs after a terrible weekend. I _must not_ eat today. |
| 9.30 | Black Coffee | Snack Bar | | | |
| 11.00 | Black Coffee | College | | | |
| 1.00 | Black Coffee | College | | | |
| 1.30 | Apple | College | * | | Feel so hungry very tempted to binge. Made myself go back to the library. |
| 3.00 | Tea | Snack Bar | | | |
| 5.00 | Tea | Snack Bar | | | Hungry |
| 5.15 | Small bar of Whole nut chocolate | On Way home | * | | Walking home couldn't stop |
| 5.20 | Mars bar × 1 | " | * | | myself from buying chocolate. |
| | Snickers bar × 1 | " | * | | Then went from Shop to Shop |
| 5.30 | Hamburgers × 2 | " | * | | eating all the way home. |
| | Bag of chips × 2 | " | * | | |
| | Bagel × 1 | | | | |
| 5.45 | 6 donuts | Home Kitchen | * | ✓ | Feel disgusted with myself. _No more food allowed today_ |
| 7.15 | Cup of tea | Kitchen | | | |
| 8.00 | Cup of Coffee | My room | | | |
| 9.00 | Slice of Toast (dry) | Kitchen | * | | Help! I can't stop eating. |
| 9.05 | Slice of toast + cheese | " | * | | I hate myself. I'm going to |
| " | 6 Slices of toast cheese/jam | " | * | | get fatter and fatter. |
| 9.20 | Bowl of Cereal × 2 | " | * | ✓ | I wish I was dead. |
| 9.40 | 4 Slices of toast and butter | " | * | ✓ L | |
| 10.15 | Cup of tea | | | L | _I will not eat tomorrow._ |

Figure 4   Example of a monitoring sheet

85

episodes should be distinguished from all other eating by marking them with a bracket (see figure 5, p. 96).

(3) The third column is for recording where the episode of eating took place. Again, you should be fairly precise about this: it is better to say 'the kitchen' than just 'home'.

(4) The fourth column, headed B, is for recording whether or not you felt the food eaten was excessive. This should be done by placing an asterisk in this column next to any item of food which you felt at the time was excessive and which you wish you had not eaten. You may regard food as excessive for one of two reasons: first, because of the *quantity* eaten (e.g. three potatoes when you felt you should have had only one); second, because of the *type* of food eaten (e.g. a chocolate bar, when you feel you ought never to eat chocolate). It is important that all food eaten in a binge is recorded on the monitoring sheet and, in such cases, each item will be asterisked.

(5) The fifth column (headed C for compensation) is for recording episodes of vomiting, and taking laxatives or diuretics. If you exercise as a method of compensating for having overeaten then this too should be recorded here.

(6) The sixth and final column is for recording how you feel at the time you eat anything, particularly after episodes of over-eating but also when you have a planned meal or snack (see Step 2, 'Instituting a Meal Plan'). This could include every-day events of life, such as having a minor argument with a friend or parent. It could be an event concerned specifically with eating, such as having been obliged by social pressure to eat something with which you were not happy. The circum-stance could also be directly related to feelings of unhappi-ness, anger, anxiety, boredom or frustration. These might be related to your eating problem, to your concerns about your weight or shape, or they may be related to other aspects of your life. If you have overeaten, it is important that you try to specify for yourself what the circumstances were in which this episode occurred and what you were feeling and thinking at

the time. This process is crucial to your coming to understand what sorts of things lead you to binge. A detailed knowledge of these factors is a major step towards intervening and overcoming your eating problems (see below under Step 3, 'Learning to Intervene'). This column should also be used for recording occasions when you weigh yourself (and how much you weigh). If you check your shape, you should record this here as well so you can get a good idea of how often this happens and what effect it has on you.

The example monitoring sheet shown in figure 4 (p. 85) is a real account of one person's eating during one day. You will see that her day began badly because she weighed herself and discovered that her weight had increased by 3 pounds over the previous weekend. In the light of this discovery she resolved not to eat at all that day. She managed not to eat until 1.30 p.m. when she had an apple. She regretted this (indicated by the asterisk) because she feared that to eat anything at all raised the chances of her losing control later. In fact she managed to avoid eating until 5.15 p.m. At this point, having felt terribly hungry all afternoon, her resolve weakened and she had a bar of chocolate. She deeply regretted this; then she completely lost control and had a full-blown binge (all items marked with an asterisk), after which she immediately made herself sick (indicated on the monitoring sheet with the letter V). She was determined not to eat anything further that day but was not successful. At nine o'clock she succumbed to the powerful urge to eat and had another binge which was followed again by vomiting (twice). She also took 10 laxative tablets (indicated on the monitoring sheet with the letter L). She was terribly upset by the loss of control and was very much afraid that her weight had consequently increased even more.

Two blank monitoring sheets are provided below. Use these to record all the food you eat over the next day or two. In this way you can refer directly to the principles you are supposed to be following, outlined in the preceding pages. Having used these two pages, *you should make your own monitoring sheets in a separate booklet, which you should then keep as a record of your progress.*

**MONITORING SHEET**

Date: _____

Day: _____

| Time | Food and liquid consumed | Place | B | C | Context of overeating/vomiting |
|------|--------------------------|-------|---|---|-------------------------------|
|      |                          |       |   |   |                               |

**MONITORING SHEET**

Date: _____

Day: _____

| Time | Food and liquid consumed | Place | B | C | Context of overeating/vomiting |
|------|--------------------------|-------|---|---|-------------------------------|
|      |                          |       |   |   |                               |

## Reviewing Your Monitoring Sheets

Once you have been monitoring your eating for a week, you should review the week as a whole and begin to try to identify any patterns in your eating. This reviewing process will continue throughout the self-help program and will provide valuable information which you will use in deciding which techniques and methods will be helpful to you in regaining control of your eating. The kinds of questions you should ask yourself at this stage include:

- Are there particular times when binges seem more likely to occur?
- Are there particular situations which tend to trigger binges?
- Are there times when eating is relatively easy to control?
- What types of food have you been eating during binges?
- Are these foods different from the types you eat at other times?
- Are there long periods of time when you eat nothing at all?
- Are these periods often followed by binges?
- Are days of strict dieting often followed by days when you binge?

These questions, continually reviewed, will provide you with a clearer understanding of the nature of your eating problem, which is crucial to your further attempts to stop binge-eating and restore your eating habits to 'normal'. It is particularly important at this stage to begin to identify times and situations when you are especially vulnerable to binge-eating. Advice on how to deal with these situations is presented in Steps 2 and 3.

*You should make a fixed appointment with yourself each week to review your monitoring sheets, record what you can learn from them, and make definite goals for the next week.* If you are seeing a helper or advocate, it is useful to take along the results of these review sessions.

**REVIEW BOX 1**

Before proceeding to Step 2, ask yourself the following questions:

*Am I writing down everything I eat on my monitoring sheets?*
   *Does this include everything I eat in binges?*
   *Am I doing this soon after having eaten?*

*Am I keeping these records systematically (that is, using a standard system of recording on standard forms)?*

*Am I reviewing my monitoring sheets regularly to try to identify patterns in my eating habits?*

If you can answer 'yes' to all these questions, you should proceed to Step 2. If you cannot answer 'yes' to these questions, you should re-read Step 1 and try again to follow all the guidelines it contains for another week or so.

# Step 2

# *Instituting a Meal Plan*

*Note: Read through all of Step 2 before beginning to try to implement the principles outlined in this section.*

The next stage of the program involves learning to eat regularly and in a controlled fashion. More specifically, it means that from now on *you must eat three meals and two or three snacks a day*. Many people, having read this, will be feeling that the prescription of a meal plan is a recipe for disaster. They will be saying to themselves: 'If I abandon my efforts to diet and start eating meals and snacks I will gain weight and inevitably get fat.' Well, of course, this would be perfectly correct if you ate meals and snacks and continued, in addition, to binge. But the meal plan is intended to displace the binges and, as a consequence, you will almost certainly be eating less overall than you were before. *It is definitely not the case that by eating regular meals you will become fat.*

## Setting Up a Meal Plan

The idea is to decide in advance exactly when you should eat and, by implication, when you should not eat. You will also have to decide what sorts of food you should eat and in what quantity. It is important at this stage that you eat according to a predetermined plan, and not according to when you feel hungry. At this early stage, *you cannot trust your sensations of hunger or fullness and they should be ignored.*

94

## Instituting a Meal Plan

*Deciding on Certain Times for Eating*
It is necessary for you to decide on a meal plan that will lay down *when* you should eat. The idea here is to decide in advance on the times when you will eat. This has a number of benefits. In particular, it permits or legitimizes eating at certain times; and it makes it explicit that at other times you are not supposed to be eating. *Once you have decided on an eating pattern it is very important that you make every effort to stick to it.* What this means is that at the times you have specified for eating, you must eat, even if you do not feel hungry and feel that you could manage to go a few more hours without eating. And during the periods between the times specified for eating, you must try your hardest to refrain from eating anything at all. *The point of all this is to replace the pattern of alternating between not eating at all and overeating with a pattern of regular eating.* For this to be successful it is necessary that there should rarely be more than a three- or four-hour gap between episodes of eating. This means that the meal plan must consist of three meals a day and two or three snacks. It is important to reiterate that once you have decided on a plan, the specified meals and snacks are not optional but obligatory; that is, *you must eat when you have planned to do so, and you must try not to eat when you have not planned to do so.* Clearly, the exact times of these meals and snacks must be tailored to your own particular circumstances; and it is probably wise to have a special plan for weekends, holidays and other times when your usual daily routine does not apply.

*A Sample Meal Plan*
The following is an example of what would constitute a sensible meal plan:

| | |
|---|---|
| 7.30 a.m. | Breakfast |
| 10.00 a.m. | Snack |
| 1.00 p.m. | Lunch |
| 4.30 p.m. | Snack |
| 7.30 p.m. | Supper |
| 10.30 p.m. | Snack |

**Plan:**
B'fast: Egg / toast
Snack: apple
Lunch: Cheese Sandwich + yogurt
Snack: Crunchy bar
Dinner: Fish, baked potato, peas, orange
Snack: apple

Date: 21st September
Day: Wednesday

| Time | Food and liquid consumed | Place | B | C | Context of overeating/ vomiting |
|------|--------------------------|-------|---|---|----------------------------------|
| 7.45 | Boiled egg, 2 slices toast<br>low fat spread<br>Cup of Tea x 2 | Kitchen | | | Egg and toast - felt like a lot to eat in one go. |
| 10.30 | Apple<br>Coffee | office | | | Not hungry but made myself have this |
| 1.00 | 2 slices bread<br>low fat Cream cheese<br>Cucumber<br>v. low fat Strawberry yogurt | Park | * | | I feel guilty, <u>all that bread</u>, feel like I'm going to gain weight. |
| 1.45 | Cup of Tea | office | | | |
| 4.00 | Cereal bar (apricot & nut)<br>Cup of Tea | office<br>Kitchen | | | Break a bit earlier than usual feel self Conscious, no-one else is eating. |
| 7.30 | Fish in parsley Sauce<br>Baked potato, peas<br>orange<br>Coffee | Kitchen | | | Ate the same as the rest of the family for the first time in ages - had a smaller portion |
| 10.30 | Cup of Tea<br>apple | Lounge | | | This is a dangerous time. I'm going straight to bed. I'm <u>not</u> going to get up. |

Figure 5   Example of a meal plan and monitoring sheet

96

You may well be alarmed by this example because it includes so many times for eating. However, it is important that your meal plan does not differ greatly from this example. The reason for this is that *such a plan is effective at displacing binge-eating because the time between episodes of planned eating is quite short.* So if ever you feel like eating when you are not supposed to do so, you can reassure yourself with the knowledge that it is not long until you will have a meal or snack. It must be stressed that each of the meals and snacks specified above would represent times when *you must eat.* As far as your monitoring is concerned, each time one of these episodes came up and you ate something in a controlled and organized fashion, you would indicate this on the sheet with a bracket. *It is important that you stick closely to the times specified on your meal plan and do not eat before a meal or snack is scheduled; and, similarly, it is important that you do not postpone or skip a meal or snack.* A typical monitoring sheet of someone who has established a meal plan (and is doing rather well) is shown in figure 5.

If you have children you will need to decide whether to eat with them or to eat separately. For some people the children's mealtime routine can provide a useful structure on which to map their own meal plans. For others, children's meals represent a major problem as a time when there is a lot of food around which they find difficult not to eat. Leftovers can be a particular problem. You must decide in advance which system is going to be most helpful to you in sticking to your meal plan.

In the box provided (p. 98), write down your meal plan: that is, the times when you should eat planned meals and snacks. The constraints of your life may make it necessary for you to have more than one plan. You may, as mentioned, need a special plan for weekends. Or there may be particular days when your work or other demands mean that you are travelling or are otherwise occupied at certain times. *You need to specify plans which will cover all these known possibilities. Remember that there should never be more than three or four hours between planned meals and snacks.*

97

**MEAL PLAN(S)**

*Deciding What Food to Include in Your Meal Plan*
It is not terribly important at this stage what you eat in your meals and snacks, as long as it is food with which you are happy: that is, food you can eat without it leading to a binge and food you can eat without having to vomit or take laxatives. This almost certainly means that it will be low-calorie food and, probably, diet food. This is not necessarily a problem, provided you are getting enough to eat. Most people with bulimia nervosa who begin a meal plan do, in fact, restrict their eating to low-calorie food and eat rather little. This can become a problem, particularly if you are rather thin, because you will be starving and unable to stick to your meal plan as a consequence. Thus, if, for example, for every meal or snack you ate a single apple, you would simply not be getting enough to eat and at some point in the day your control would break down and you would binge. It is, therefore, important, as already noted, that you get enough to eat.

What constitutes 'enough' is likely to be a problem for many people. There are three ways of dealing with this difficulty. The first is a simple matter of seeing what is happening to your eating: if you are trying to stick to a program of three meals and three snacks a day, and you find that an hour or so after your lunchtime meal you feel like a binge, then it might be the case that you are physiologically deprived and your lunches are too small. It is clear that in such circumstances, if you increased the amount you ate for lunch, you would not feel hungry before the next scheduled snack and would be less likely to lose control and binge. A second strategy is to use someone else as a reference point. That is, choose a friend or relative who you feel is a 'normal' eater, and examine the quantities she eats in a meal. This might help you get an idea of how you should change how much you include in your meals. The third strategy is to buy some (non-diet) prepared meals for one from a supermarket as a guideline to how much food a meal should contain. As part of this process of deciding how much to eat you might even discuss the problem with a trusted friend or relative (see the section on 'Talking to Someone' in Step 3). Or you could discuss it with your helper/advocate.

It is common for people at this stage to have considerable difficulty knowing what foods to include in their meal plan. The

99

important point here is to *try to eat only what you are happy with*. You should avoid eating anything which you know will be likely to trigger a binge. This may well mean that you are the only person not having a second helping or not having a dessert. This can be embarrassing, but at least you will have the satisfaction of knowing you have stuck to your meal plan and not gone on to binge.

*Planning the Content of Meals and Snacks in Advance*
Deciding what to eat can be a problem, particularly when you are feeling hungry. *It is advisable, therefore, to plan in advance what you are going to eat.* Some people find that this is best done immediately before a meal or snack; others find it helpful to sketch out a plan before going to bed at night. A good method is to use the back or top of your monitoring sheet for planning the next day's eating (fig. 5, p. 96). You will then be able to check how you are doing as you fill in the sheet throughout the day. If it is difficult for you to specify exactly what you will have for each meal or snack, put down a few limited alternatives with which you will be happy. You will have to discover whether planning immediately before a meal or a day in advance is best for you.

*Ending a Meal*
*It is useful to remove all decisions about your eating from the actual time when you are eating.* Planning meals and snacks ahead of time, as advised above, is one way of doing this. Another is to decide before you begin a meal exactly how much you are going to have. This can be helpful because otherwise it is easy to find that you have eaten more than you are happy with and then feel that you might as well go on and binge. A useful strategy here is to set out your meal or snack before you and decide that one item (say, a piece of fruit) will be the 'full stop' to the meal. When you have eaten the 'full stop', the meal is over.

*Sticking to the Plan No Matter What*
*It is essential that you stick to the decisions that you have made in advance.* If, having eaten your 'full stop', you think that you still feel hungry, you must try to ignore this feeling and abide by your

decision not to eat any more. The reason for this is that your feelings of hunger or fullness cannot be relied upon; and if you do modify your eating plan in the light of these feelings your eating will soon become disorganized again. Perhaps the plan you devised in advance was wrong in certain respects and ought to be changed. However, it is generally unwise to make changes as the day proceeds. Rather, you can make a new plan for the following day having learned from the mistakes of today. Indeed, it is useful to examine your monitoring sheet at the end of each day to see what you can learn from it about the particular meal plan you devised and any difficulties in sticking to it that you may have encountered. This can help you improve the plan for the next day.

*Introducing a Meal Plan in Stages*
In rare cases, for some people who are fasting for long periods or who binge repeatedly throughout the day, the idea of instituting a meal plan for the entire day is too daunting a prospect. In these circumstances it is best to divide the day up into three or four chunks and begin by instituting an eating plan just for the easiest chunk (usually the morning). Once order is restored to this first segment and you are able to stick to a plan, you can then concentrate on the next least difficult part of the day, and so on.

## Dealing with Problems

Once you decide on an appropriate meal plan for you, do not assume that you will immediately be able to stick to it. You are almost certain to run into difficulties. The aim of the exercise at this stage is for you gradually to reduce the times of difficulty so that binge-eating becomes less and less frequent and normal meals and snacks become more and more the norm. And by examining your monitoring sheet at the end of the day you can learn from your mistakes and make changes to your future plans. *Whatever has happened on a particular day, it is essential that you begin the following day afresh, committed to your meal plan for that day.*

101

## When Things Go Wrong

If you run into difficulties during the day you will probably feel tempted to abandon all effort to adhere to your plan for the rest of that day. For example, you may be offered a piece of cake, eat it (when you should not have done so because it was not planned) and then go on to binge; and then immediately resolve not to eat at all for the rest of the day to compensate for having overeaten. This is a grave mistake and will almost certainly lead to further overeating. *The important thing to do when something goes wrong is to get yourself back on your plan as soon as possible.* So, assuming, in the example above, that the cake that led to a binge was offered at four o'clock, the right way to proceed is to resolve to eat the meal planned for supper. This may seem silly when you have just overeaten, but getting back on to the plan is your only real protection against further episodes of loss of control. Of course this is going to be extremely difficult and when you have overeaten the temptation to diet or to fast is likely to be very strong. *This temptation must be fought and overcome. To give in and cut back on your eating is to undermine the value of the meal plan.* The most you should allow yourself to do is to sit down in advance of the meal with your meal plan and replace certain filling items (like a sandwich or baked potato) with lighter, less filling food (like fruit or yogurt). Even this process of making substitutions in your meal plan can be dangerous, because the urge not to eat at all could be very strong and you may be tempted to replace the entire meal with, say, a few grapes. This will not work. The important thing here is to have the meal and for that meal to be a genuine one.

It is often very difficult to follow this advice, especially after a full-blown binge. At such times you are likely to feel disgusted and ashamed with yourself, and to feel particularly acutely the loneliness of trying to sort your problems out on your own. Although it is, of course, terribly difficult to do so, it is important that you find a way of picking yourself up and carrying on. It might be helpful at such times to ask yourself: *'Have I made any progress at all? Because if I have, then, however bad I feel at this moment, it is this progress which is really important.'*

It is inevitable that there will be slip-ups in the course of your making progress towards recovery. And they will make you very unhappy; at times, they might make you feel hopeless about ever really changing. But, *if you do not allow such slip-ups to over-whelm you, it is possible to learn from them and to move forward.* It is particularly useful to discuss these slip-ups with a helper, and to talk about your reaction to them, and how you can learn from them.

*Dealing with Disruptions*
There will be occasions when, through no fault of your own, your plans for the day are disrupted. For example, just before you sit down to have lunch, a friend arrives and insists that you accompany her to a restaurant. The way to cope with this is to accept that, from time to time, your plan will have to be revised in the light of unexpected events. Try not to panic when this happens, but instead take a moment to yourself to make changes to your plan for the rest of the day on the basis of the new developments. In general, you should try to change as little as possible, so that the revised plan remains close to your original plan.

*Dealing with Special Occasions*
Special occasions will arise when you will not be able to stick to your usual plan. You may be obliged to go to a wedding reception, or you may be taken out to dinner by friends or parents, and so on. It is not always possible to avoid such circumstances and, although it is best to be fairly strict about adhering to your meal plan, especially in the early weeks, such occasions can present you with a useful exercise. In such circumstances, although your normal plan will not be appropriate, it is essential that you do have *some* plan for that particular day, and that the plan is as close to your usual meal plan as possible.

It is a bad idea to attempt to deal with a special evening occasion by fasting throughout the day. It might seem like the safest strategy, given that you know you will be eating a large meal in the evening. But it would be far better to make a minor adjustment to your routine by, say, planning to eat as usual until

103

the special evening meal, planning to have only a starter and a main course at that meal (choosing light food with which you will feel comfortable), and, given that the meal is likely to go on for a rather long time, planning to skip the late evening snack. It is essential that you do not attempt to eat less the following day because of the previous evening's meal: you should immediately return to your normal meal plan. If you try to compensate by eating less it is very likely that at some point in the day you will binge. It is worth remembering that *no one meal can have a significant effect on your weight*.

*Dealing with Vomiting*
The purpose of establishing a meal plan is to displace binge-eating with 'normal' eating. For most people, as this becomes increasingly successful, the number of times they feel it necessary to make themselves sick will correspondingly decrease. If you don't binge you won't feel the need to vomit. For this reason, it is often not necessary to direct any special attention at trying to stop vomiting.

There are two exceptions to this. Some people find that on occasion, even when they have stuck to their meal plan and eaten exactly what they planned to eat, they feel full, perhaps even bloated, and they become anxious that if they don't vomit they will become fat. If this happens you must try to resist the urge to vomit. Remember that *vomiting encourages overeating and will therefore work against your efforts to stop binge-eating*. If you experience such feelings and fears, it is important to try to distract yourself until the urge to vomit has passed. The first time you do this it may take some time for the urge to vomit to pass; but, if you do resist this urge, the next time it arises it will pass more quickly and after a while the urge will disappear altogether. You must experiment with what sorts of distractions work best for you. Most people find that activities like reading or listening to music are not helpful. In fact, apart from going for a walk, which some people do find helpful, solitary activities are probably best avoided if possible. Being with people can have a calming effect and also makes it difficult to escape to vomit.

The second exception concerns those people who get into the

habit of vomiting not only after a binge, but after eating
anything at all. If this is what you do it is essential that, in
addition to establishing a meal plan, you work towards eliminating vomiting altogether. Some people can manage this by
simply saying to themselves: 'I shall only include in my planned
meals and snacks the sort of food I am prepared not to vomit, in
the sort of quantities I am prepared to hold down.' Other people
find achieving this end more difficult and if you are one of them
it is best to proceed more gradually. Divide the day up into six
chunks (early morning, late morning, early afternoon, late
afternoon, early evening, late evening). Ask yourself during
which of these would it be easiest (or least difficult) to eat
the planned meal or snack without vomiting. Once you have
made this decision, you should eat without vomiting during this
time. Use the same sort of distractions as those described above
for coping when you have eaten. Once you can eat regularly
without vomiting during this chunk of time you should decide
which is the next easiest time and eat the planned meal or snack
without vomiting during this time (as well as during the time
you have already eliminated vomiting). In this way vomiting
should be gradually eliminated altogether.

*Preoccupation with Food*
A common complaint of people who are putting a lot of effort
into planning ahead and trying to stick to a meal plan is that they
find that they are having to think about food and eating even
more than they did when their eating was completely out of
control. In a sense, they complain, the treatment is making them
feel worse! This can be distressing but it should not be a cause
for real concern because it is a phase which passes in a matter of
a few weeks. It is simply the case that, if your eating habits have
become very disorganized, to restore them to normal it is
necessary, for a period of time, for eating to occupy a particularly important place in your life.

*Preoccupation with Weight and Shape*
Many people who begin eating according to a meal plan of the
sort described above also find that they become increasingly

concerned about their weight and their shape. They are convinced that they are gaining weight and they feel fat. This is an understandable reaction in someone who has previously been attempting to eat very little. However, if you find that you react in this way, it is important to remember that it is *a psychological reaction to the change in your eating habits rather than a genuine signal of what is happening to your weight and shape.* You will regularly be checking your weight, so you will be able to confirm that replacing binges with regular meals and snacks is not in fact causing you to gain weight or become fat. These concerns and preoccupations will gradually diminish as you become more confident of your control over eating.

## What Is a 'Good Day'?

It is important to be clear about what constitutes a 'good day'. Until now you may well have seen as a 'good day' one in which you have been able to avoid eating altogether or, perhaps, managed not to overeat. However, once you establish a meal plan, a 'good day' is one in which you have been able to stick to your plan. You may have a constant struggle throughout an entire day fighting urges to binge when you were not supposed to be eating, forcing yourself to eat planned meals when you desperately wanted to fast, and resisting the urge to vomit; and, at the end of such a day you may feel exhausted and demoralized. However, if, despite the great struggle, you were able to stick to your meal plan, eat what you were supposed to eat at the scheduled times, and avoid eating in between scheduled times, then that day was a 'good day' – a personal triumph, in fact. And the more such 'good days' you have, the easier sticking to the meal plan will become.

It is important to add here that if you have one or two slip-ups during a particular day, this does not mean that the day has been 'ruined', and it is important for you not to see it in this way. If you regard an unscheduled bar of chocolate, for example, as a total disaster, there is a risk that you might be tempted to abandon your attempts at control altogether, feeling that the day has already become a 'bad day', so you might as well binge and start afresh the next day. *This is a very common trap and one which you must avoid.* If you find that you tend to think in terms of 'good days' and 'bad days', you might find it helpful to think of each day as being divided into smaller sections or units. Thus, the period between breakfast and the morning snack could be regarded as one unit, that between the morning snack and lunch as a second unit, and so on. Each unit during which you manage to keep control can then be viewed as a separate achievement. It will be apparent that a slip-up in the early afternoon has only 'spoiled' one of the six or so sections of the day; and if you can then return immediately to your plan for the rest of the day, as advised, you will still have had five 'good' sections out of six, which is certainly not a 'bad day'.

---

**REVIEW BOX 2**

Before proceeding to Step 3, ask yourself the following questions:

*Have I decided on a meal plan; that is, on definite times when I should eat meals and snacks?*

*Have I been planning what to eat at these times?*

*Have I been making sensible modifications to my meal plan to deal with special situations (e.g. holidays, weekends)?*

*Have I tried to stick to my meal plan every day (without necessarily ever completely succeeding)?*

*Have I been trying to get back to my meal plan when things have gone wrong?*

*Have I attempted not to vomit after eating my planned meals and snacks?*

If you can answer 'yes' to all these questions, you should proceed with Step 3. If you cannot answer 'yes' to these questions, you should re-read Step 2 and try again to follow all the guidelines it contains.

# Step 3

# *Learning to Intervene to Prevent Binge-Eating*

*Note: Read through all of Step 3 before beginning to try to implement the principles outlined in this section.*

If you are trying to stick to a meal plan you have already gone some way towards replacing binge-eating with 'normal' eating habits. However, it is likely that it will, at times, be very difficult for you to stick to this plan; and it is also likely that, at times, you will have a powerful urge to binge. It is essential that you develop strategies for dealing with these difficulties. This section contains a number of suggestions designed to help you both in your efforts to stick to your meal plan and in your attempts to resist the urge to binge.

## Talking to Someone

Establishing a meal plan and attempting to stick to it can be a formidably difficult task. It is asking a very great deal of yourself to expect to be able to manage this entirely on your own, even with the assistance of a detached helper/advocate whom you consult for advice and support. *It can be enormously helpful to enlist also the assistance of a close friend or relative.* This is not because they can then take control and make all the decisions. No one can take over this task and do it for you. But they can help by providing you with very particular kinds of practical assistance. For example, it can be a great help to arrange to have some of your evening meals with someone else and to spend time with them afterwards. Also, if you know that it is going to be difficult for you to resist eating at a particular time (when you are not supposed to eat), it can be helpful to arrange to spend time with someone else. Similarly, if you can drop in on someone or telephone them when you are feeling particularly like binge-eating, this can see you through a difficult time.

Now, of course, much of this can be achieved without confiding the real reason why you are seeking companionship. However, the secrecy and deceit that is so often such a major part of the lives of people who binge is a great burden which itself causes much misery. It can be a considerable relief to tell someone of your troubles and not have to keep up the constant deception. Also, someone who knows of your particular difficulties can be much more help to you than someone who does not. You may well feel extremely apprehensive about telling anyone about your problems with eating for fear that they would not understand and would think poorly of you. If you choose someone you respect and trust this really is most unlikely. It is a sad fact that almost all women within our culture are concerned about their weight and shape, and a great many have problems of some kind with eating. It is not at all difficult for them to see how such problems can become more serious. Almost invariably the people in whom one confides are anxious to be as helpful as they can be. If this is hard for you to accept, think of a good friend and ask yourself how you would react if she came to you in distress and confided some personal difficulty (say, that she was secretly drinking excessively or was shop-lifting) and think how you would react. Surely it is reasonable for you to expect as much acceptance and sympathy as you would be prepared to give.

*It is important to stress that the assistance such a friend or relative can provide you with is quite different from the help you could get from an outsider whom you consult as an independent advocate or helper.*


## Planning Ahead

However resolved you are and however much forethought you put into it, it is not easy to stick to a meal plan. Many things can happen during a day to disrupt your plan and sometimes you will feel unable to stick to your good intentions. It is very common for people who binge to think that once something goes wrong with their eating there is nothing they can do to intervene – a binge is inevitable. In fact there is a great deal that you can do to intervene and such intervention is possible at all stages in the process. So, spending time planning ahead, spotting potential hazards and taking some form of evasive action, and recognizing the urge to binge early in the process and having a plan for what to do about it, are all forms of intervention which are effective at preventing binge-eating. Whilet it may be hard to believe at this stage, it is even possible to stop a binge once you have started.

There are a number of simple measures you should take to make the task of sticking to a meal plan easier for you. A complete list could be endless, but the following are some of the main tactics people find useful:

(1) *Restrict eating to one or two specified areas within the house,* such as the kitchen and the dining room. The areas where you usually binge (typically some private space, such as the bedroom) should be designated as places where food is never allowed. If you usually binge in the kitchen, it would be best if you found somewhere else to eat and never ate anything at all in the kitchen. If you find it impossible not to 'pick' at food while you cook, keep some chewing gum handy in the kitchen and when you feel like picking chew gum instead. If you only have one room available to you, then designate a particular area for eating meals and snacks (such as a particular chair or place at table) and eat there and nowhere else.

(2) When you do eat, *eat slowly*. Do not do anything else while you are eating like reading or watching television.

(3) Before eating a meal, *plan exactly what you will do when the meal is finished*.

(4) *Restrict your supplies of food*. Buy food in small quantities and do not keep large supplies of food readily available.

(5) *When shopping for food have a list of what you are going to buy. Do not shop for food when you feel hungry or think that*

*you are likely to binge.* If shopping is a particularly difficult time for you, arrange to shop with someone else. When you are planning to shop for particular items do not carry with you more money than necessary or credit cards.

(6) *Do not leave leftover food lying around.* In fact, it is far better to throw leftovers away than for them to represent a threat to your control over your eating. This may feel wasteful and wrong; but it is better to be wasteful as a temporary way of helping yourself recover than not to be wasteful and thereby to make it impossible for you to stop binge-eating.

(7) *Do not allow anyone to bully you into eating anything you do not want.* It is very common for people to try and press food upon you (e.g. *'Do have another helping of dessert'* or *'Go on: have a slice of delicious chocolate cake. I made it specially for you'*). It is, at times, difficult to refuse such offers without being rude. However, it is possible to be firm and polite in sticking to what you want to do (e.g. *'No thank you. It was delicious but I couldn't manage any more'* or *'No thank you. I won't have anything because I have just eaten'* or *'I shall be eating later and I don't want to spoil my appetite'*). If you are particularly plagued by the tyranny of others trying to force you to eat, you might find it helpful to rehearse two or three such phrases which you can then produce when required.

(8) Finally, as pointed out earlier, in attempting to follow a plan for the day, it is important to *take each moment separately.* It is very common for people to say: *'Well, I got that one wrong, so I might as well abandon any attempt to eat normally for the rest of the day.'* Indeed, it is essential if something goes wrong that you go back to your plan and see what it is that you are supposed to do next. If you can get back on to your plan immediately and stick to it for the rest of the day then you know that you have made real progress.

Most of the measures you must take to prevent yourself running into difficulties, or to extricate yourself from situations which have become problematic, you will have to work out for yourself by examining your monitoring sheets and seeing what situations are particularly difficult for you, and what tactics you find most helpful. Similarly, by paying careful attention to the circumstances in which you do lose control and binge, you can see what sorts of situations are particularly problematic for you and require special attention. *It is important for you to be one step ahead of trouble.* Planning the next day's meals and snacks ahead of time is part of this process. But you can be even more focused in planning ahead and try to spot particular episodes or circumstances which are likely to lead to your overeating. You can do this by examining your monitoring sheets. It is likely that, after a week or two of monitoring, certain patterns will become obvious to you. You may find that you invariably binge after particular events, such as going shopping or being on your own with no particular plans or appointments; this knowledge allows you to anticipate when you are likely to run into difficulty and to adapt arrangements to make things easier for you. So, for example, if you find that you invariably binge when you are unpacking the shopping, you could arrange for a friend to be around at this time.

### Be Sensible with Alcohol

It is very common for people to find that their eating is particularly difficult to control after they have been drinking because alcohol tends to undermine the resolve to control eating. If this is true for you it will be very apparent from your monitoring sheets. The solution is a simple one: either drink in moderation or, if this is difficult for you, do not drink at all. You should be very strict about this while your prime goal is attempting to restore order to your eating habits. Once you are no longer binge-eating and are confident of your control, you can review this matter and decide when it would be safe to drink and how much you can drink without alcohol becoming a problem for you. It must be stressed that *if you drink excessively you will not be able to make full use of this program and it is unlikely that you will be able to overcome your problems with eating*.

## Intervening in the Moment

*It is important to have plans prepared for what you will do if things go wrong.* For example, you may well have an urge to eat just after you have finished one of your planned meals or snacks. *It is very useful to have a list of things you could do instead of eating* (like going for a walk, having a bath, telephoning a friend, etc.); and when you feel an urge to eat you would then start working your way through the list until the urge passed. It is common for people to say: *'If I have a strong urge to binge, however long I postpone it, in the end I will succumb.'* They feel that it is almost as if the binge has a will of its own and that in the end, if it is lurking, it will get them. In fact, if you do intervene and prevent a binge, the urge to eat does pass; and, of course, it is soon time for a planned meal or snack when eating is quite legitimate. Intervening in this way is not easy. At first it might even seem impossible. But you can be reassured that *each time you do intervene successfully you make intervening in the future that much easier.* And the more often you intervene successfully the less often the urge to binge will arise.

You must give careful attention to the preparation of your list of things to do in order to overcome the urge to binge and delay eating until the next meal or snack. This list can include any activity which you feel might help in this regard, but the following guidelines may be useful:

(1) The activity should be easy to do at times when you might feel an urge to eat.
(2) Activities which involve using your hands are helpful, e.g. knitting, sewing, handiwork, gardening, playing a musical instrument, etc. More passive activities, such as watching television, or activities which require mental concentration, such as reading a book, are unlikely to be effective in blocking out thoughts of food.
(3) Activities which remove you from your habitual eating places, like the kitchen, are often useful in emergencies. These would include outdoor activities such as going for a walk or a bicycle ride.

(4) At some level you may regard eating as a treat or indulgence, so it is a good idea to include in your list activities which you regard as self-indulgent, such as going to the movies in the afternoon, buying yourself a new item of clothing or a bunch of flowers, or telephoning a friend you seldom see. Often something as simple as a long hot bath using scented bath oil can make you feel better about yourself.

(5) Do not include on your list activities which you actually dislike. It is very important that your distracting activities are not tasks or duties which you will not actually want to do. So, it is generally not advisable to include things like scrubbing the kitchen floor or going for a long run, unless you actually enjoy doing these things. A sense of virtuous achievement is not what you are aiming for here; rather, you are looking for a way to see yourself through a difficult period until it is a scheduled time for you to eat again.

The list you do make can obviously be added to or subtracted from as you try out the effectiveness of your activities in various situations. It is a good idea to carry the list with you, so that when you feel an urge to eat you can immediately consult it and decide which of the activities you might use in that particular circumstance to tide you over until the next meal or snack time. The two pages that follow are provided for you to write in your list. Use the first page to write in a provisional list; you should amend this as you gain experience of what does and does not work for you. Once you are confident of what the most effective activities are, write them down on the second page as your updated list. You can always update the list again if you discover anything particularly effective later.

**PROVISIONAL LIST OF ACTIVITIES**

**UPDATED LIST OF ACTIVITIES**

## REVIEW BOX 3

Before proceeding to Step 4, ask yourself the following questions:

*Have I been avoiding, wherever possible, those situations which I have identified as ones in which I am likely to binge?*

*Have I regularly been planning ahead in an effort to be 'one step ahead of trouble'?*

*When things have gone wrong and I have been on the verge of a binge, have I been attempting to intervene?*

*Have I been systematically working through a list of activities in an effort to delay and prevent binge-eating?*

*Have I been able on some occasions to prevent a binge from happening, either by careful planning or by actively intervening?*

If you can answer *'yes'* to all of the above questions, you should proceed to the next step. If you cannot answer *'yes'* to these questions, you should re-read Step 3 and try again to follow all the guidelines it contains.

# Step 4

# *Problem Solving*

*Note: Read through all of Step 4 before beginning to try to implement the principles outlined in this section.*

It is very common for people with difficulties controlling their eating to binge in response to all sorts of problems which overwhelm them. These problems can concern issues to do with food and eating as well as with countless other aspects of life, such as work, family, friends and so on. It is important that you develop a strategy for identifying problems, addressing them and generating solutions other than eating. Sometimes the identification of the problem is easy: you might see, when making plans for the next day, that some event represents a potential obstacle to your meal plan. For example, a friend you have not seen for a long time has announced that she will drop round and you feel you should make something special for the occasion; or you know you will be extremely nervous because of a job interview in the afternoon and will not feel like eating all day. At other times identifying the problem will be more difficult. You may feel anxious or miserable and know that this makes you vulnerable to the impulse to overeat. It is easy in such cases to identify the problem as an urge to overeat, when the real problem is whatever it is that is making you feel anxious or depressed. For many people with eating problems the urge to overeat is an automatic response to problems of any kind. When such an urge arises, it is therefore important to ask the question: *'Why do I have an urge to overeat now? What is the problem that lies behind this feeling?'* Of course, the answer to this question often will

118

have been that you have not eaten enough (or at all). But if you are sticking to your meal plan and eating a reasonable amount of food, then there must be some other answer. *It is important for you to try to identify what the basic problem is.* Once you have done so you will be in a position to deal with the problem and you will not then automatically overeat. The steps shown below should be followed in helping you deal with the problem.

## The Five Steps in Problem Solving

(1) Write the problem out as clearly as you can on your monitoring sheet. If there is more than one problem, try to untangle the problems into separate ones; then deal with these individually.

(2) Produce as many solutions to the problem as you can think of. You can be quite uninhibited about this because you want to be able to look at all possible solutions.

(3) Examine each of your possible solutions and think about its implications: that is, precisely what would be involved, whether you realistically could see it through, and whether it is likely to be effective.

(4) Choose what looks to you like being the best solution (or combination of solutions) and decide to act on it.

(5) At the end of the day, review what has happened and consider whether your solution was effective. If it did not work out as it was supposed to, try to think what you might have done to produce a better outcome.

Problem solving as described above may look rather tedious and somewhat complicated. However, it is a highly effective technique and, with a little practice, it can be managed quite easily. Figure 6 (p. 120) shows two examples of problems someone identified and the solutions she generated, together with a statement of the outcome or 'evaluation'.

For some people problem solving in the way described above comes very easily. It is largely a formalization of what they have been doing in a rough way before. For them, the benefits of doing the problem solving more formally, in the way described

| (a) Food-related problem: evening meal with friend cancelled at last moment | (b) Non-food-related problem: left house keys at work |
|---|---|
| 1 *Problem*: What am I going to do about eating? | 1 *Problem*: Feeling panicky (and like eating) because I don't know how I am going to get in. |
| 2 *Alternative solutions*:<br>(a) eat at home – leftover food<br>(b) eat at home – get take-out<br>(c) avoid eating altogether<br>(d) arrange to eat with friends | 2 *Alternative solutions*:<br>(a) return to work to get keys<br>(b) break in window at back of house<br>(c) wait outside until others return<br>(d) visit friend and return later<br>(e) leave note on door |
| 3 *Implications*:<br>(a) OK, could treat myself to a drink<br>(b) raining – take-out too large<br>(c) too much restraint, probably end up overeating<br>(d) would be a good way to spend the evening | 3 *Implications*:<br>(a) probably no one left at work so will not be able to get in<br>(b) a bit drastic, too expensive to repair<br>(c) it may be a very long wait in the cold<br>(d) would be good to visit Sue, hope she's in<br>(e) good idea, leave possible phone numbers of where I'll be |
| 4 *Decision*: Do (d) and if that's not possible will do (a) | 4 *Decision*: Will do (d) and (e) |
| 5 *Evaluation*: Friends couldn't make it – had leftovers and drink, successful | 5 *Evaluation*: Sue not in, visited Steve instead, Clare saw my note and phoned within an hour to say she was home. Felt good, hadn't panicked and hadn't eaten. |

Figure 6    Example of problem solving

above, will be obvious and they will experience these benefits rapidly. For others, formal problem solving is something quite alien to their way of thinking and behaving; and they are likely to struggle to use this technique effectively.

## Problem Solving

The following blank pages headed 'Problem Solving' are for you to try to use the problem-solving technique in the way described. Over the course of the next week, on two occasions identify a problem and try to come to a resolution, using the spaces provided. Then take these to your 'helper' and talk them over together. This discussion can be especially useful if you have gone through a problem-solving exercise and it has *not* worked. You will then be able to look at what options you might have considered and how this might have affected the outcome.

### Problems with Depression

Feeling depressed can be a major obstacle to overcoming eating difficulties. People sometimes react to relatively minor setbacks in their efforts to deal with their eating problems by becoming totally demoralized and fiercely self-critical. As a result, their confidence and strength of purpose are undermined and they find it even harder to control their eating. It is important to accept that overcoming your problems with eating is likely to be a struggle and that you will inevitably not succeed all the time in everything you are trying to do. *If you succeed at something you are making some progress and you should give yourself credit for this*; and where you do not succeed you can learn something which can help you in the future.

Sometimes more general feelings of depression, not specifically related to eating or weight concerns, also lower morale and make it hard to control eating. If it is apparent from your monitoring sheets that this represents a pattern, you should try to think what it is that is making you feel depressed. Treat it as a 'problem' in the manner described above and try to find solutions. You might find a self-help book useful, such as Ivy Blackburn's *Coping with Depression* or David Burns's *Feeling Good*.*

Occasionally, people are so depressed that they are seriously incapacitated. They do not sleep properly; wake up early in the morning; feel tired all the time and completely without energy; find concentrating impossible because of their preoccupation

---

*Ivy Blackburn, *Coping with Depression*, Chambers, 1987; David D. Burns, *Feeling Good: The New Mood Therapy*, New York, Signet, 1981.

## **PROBLEM SOLVING**

PROBLEM:

ALTERNATIVE SOLUTIONS:

IMPLICATIONS:

DECISION:

EVALUATION:

## PROBLEM SOLVING

PROBLEM:

ALTERNATIVE SOLUTIONS:

IMPLICATIONS:

DECISION:

EVALUATION:

with gloomy thoughts and are consequently unable to work; they cannot see any hope in the future for themselves and life to them does not seem worth living. *If you are feeling persistently this depressed it is important that you go and talk to your doctor soon.* You can get help; if you do, your mood will improve and you will then be able to make use of this manual and deal with your eating problems.

## Problems with Relationships

It is common for people who are monitoring their eating to find that binges are triggered by problems in their relationships with their parents, husbands or boyfriends, or other close friends. If you find that this is the case for you, it is worthwhile trying to deal with this area as a 'problem' in the way described above and trying to specify exactly what the nature of the difficulty is and what you can do about it. Often a pattern emerges from the monitoring sheets which makes it clear where the problem lies. It could be something very specific, like your mother unwittingly forcing you to eat food you do not want; or it might concern a more general issue with parents, such as difficulties with independence. Similarly, with a husband or boyfriend it could relate to something concerning eating, or some more general aspect of your relationship. There are, of course, any number of possibilities here. *The point is that by writing down what the nature of the problem is and by thinking about what sorts of solutions might be possible, you create the possibility of breaking a cycle.* You may even decide that your relationship problems are of such importance that you should seek professional help in resolving them.

## Problems with Feeling Fat

It is very common for people who have difficulties controlling their eating to report that they feel fat, and that this feeling makes them diet; but at the same time, feeling fat distresses them and makes them want to eat. Most people do not question this feeling. It regularly occurs and they assume that it is a

124

feeling which is a genuine reflection of the state of their body. However, if you record on your monitoring sheet every time you have a strong sense of feeling fat, it is likely that you will discover an interesting fact: namely, that this feeling arises in all sorts of different contexts, some of which are clearly related to circumstances surrounding food (such as after having eaten a meal) or shape (such as wearing a tight dress or going out with a thin friend), but many of which have nothing at all to do with food or eating. *In fact, you may well discover that, like so many people whose eating is out of control, for you 'feeling fat' has come to constitute an automatic response to any negative emotion.* You may just feel 'bad' and immediately convert this into feeling 'fat'. But there are many events or circumstances which could be responsible for your feeling bad and they should be recognized for what they are and addressed and resolved. The way to proceed is to record on your monitoring sheet whenever you feel fat and ask yourself: '*What is the real problem that is making me feel bad?*' Once the problem has been identified you will be in a position to think about appropriate solutions.

## Problems With Feeding Other People

Preparing food for friends or relatives and eating with them should be a pleasurable experience. But it can be a nightmare for people with bulimia nervosa. All sorts of basic issues cause anxiety and confusion, such as: 'What shall I cook?', 'How much should I prepare?', 'Do I serve everyone's food myself or do I leave them to do it for themselves?', 'What size helpings should I serve?', 'Do I offer second helpings and, if so, how forcefully?', 'How long should the meal take?', 'What do I do with leftover food?' These questions all pose serious problems which need solving in the way described above.

Two general principles might be helpful. First, try to avoid doing anything which you know will create difficulties for you. So, if you are preparing a special three-course meal and including a conventional dessert would be a problem, why not prepare some exotic fruit instead? And, if leftovers are going to be difficult for you to resist, arrange for someone else to remove them or, if this is not possible, throw them away. Second, as a general rule it is a good idea to treat others as you would like to be treated yourself. So, for example, do not force food on to people and give them as much choice about what is going to happen as possible.

---

### REVIEW BOX 4

Before proceeding to the next step, ask yourself the following questions:

*Have I been identifying problems which make me feel upset (e.g., sad, anxious, angry), or like binge-eating, and been writing them down?*

*Have I been using problem-solving techniques as a way of trying to deal effectively with these problems?*

*Have I found that by writing down the problem and attempting to solve it, on some occasions, I am able to deal with difficulties which in the past would have led to binges?*

If you are able to answer 'yes' to all of these questions, you should proceed to the next section. If you cannot answer 'yes' to these questions, you should re-read Step 4 and try again to follow the guidelines it contains.

---

# Step 5

# *Eliminating Dieting*

*Note: Read through all of Step 5 before beginning to try to implement the principles outlined in this section.*

It is possible that you will have managed to stick to your meal plan by eating a fairly skimpy diet. So, you may well be managing to stick to three meals and two or three snacks a day and in this context you may well have stopped binge-eating or reduced it to an occasional occurrence. But your control will remain precarious while you are only eating small quantities of low-calorie food. It is also the case that the effort involved in sticking to such a regime will mean that the degree to which you are preoccupied with thoughts about food and eating will not diminish and may even increase. *It is essential to your continued progress that you make a real effort at reducing your tendency to diet.*

## The Three Ways of Dieting

There are essentially three ways in which people diet:

(1) Simply trying not to eat: that is, going for long periods without eating, even to the point of fasting for days. The establishment of your meal plan will have eliminated this.
(2) Attempting to eat very little (e.g., eating less than 1000 calories a day). This method of dieting will have to go if you are to be sure of avoiding binges.
(3) Eliminating from your diet particular foods which are high in calories or which you feel make you binge. This method

will also have to go because, as long as you retain the concept of 'bad' foods, or 'forbidden' foods, or 'banned' foods, or 'dangerous' foods, or 'binge' foods, or whatever you call them, you will be vulnerable to binge-eating under certain circumstances.

You should not attempt to deal with your desire to diet until you have managed to establish a regular meal plan and it has had a significant impact on normalizing your eating habits. This could take anything from two weeks to a few months, depending on the point from which you started. No definite guideline can be provided here but, as a rule of thumb, if you are sticking to your meal plan and not binge-eating on most days you are probably ready to start tackling the dieting.

### Fasting

The meal plan has dealt with the first method of dieting: that is, fasting will have been eliminated by your eating regular meals and snacks.

### Eating too Little

It is often very difficult for someone who has been attempting to restrict the amount they eat for some time to have any idea of what constitutes a 'normal' amount of food. In fact, people vary considerably in how much food they require and no strict guidelines can be provided which would apply to everyone. It is preferable, therefore, that you experiment and discover for yourself what is right for you. Initially, it could be helpful to ask someone for assistance. Earlier it was suggested that examining how much others eat could help. This is certainly true. However, it is even better if you can talk to someone you trust about this and seek their advice and assistance. Better still is to arrange to have meals with them, as suggested above, and use these occasions as an opportunity to discover what constitutes a reasonable amount of food.

A word of caution must be added here. Many women diet and it would not help you to try to copy the eating habits of someone who is restricting her eating. In choosing a friend with whom to discuss this matter and possibly with whom you might eat, try to find someone who is not overly concerned about her weight and who is not dieting.

It would be a mistake to try to deal with the problem of deciding how much to eat by trying to follow some exact formula. In the end you must come to know what amounts are right for each meal and snack. For many people the prospect of such knowledge might seem an impossibility, and they may well feel that some guidance, at least at this early stage, is essential. In order to help them, *as a very rough guide*, an account of three days of 'normal' eating is given in figure 7 (p. 130). The amount of food eaten is roughly what an average weight woman who is eating normally would eat. The relative proportions of fat, carbohydrate and protein are also typical of someone whose eating habits are perfectly normal. These examples are merely illustrative and *you should definitely not attempt to copy them*. You may well need to eat more than shown in the examples and you should not be alarmed if this is the case.

*Avoiding Particular Types of Food*
An examination of your monitoring sheets will reveal that the foods you eat in a binge are usually those very foods you are especially attempting to exclude from your diet because they are 'fattening' or because you think that they trigger binges. It is very common for people to say '*I never eat chocolate*' and then to discover that their binges contain a variety of chocolate bars. It is important that you come to be able to eat in moderation those foods you are avoiding, so that ultimately you can make a rational choice about what you want to eat. If you continue to avoid particular 'trigger' foods, there will always be the threat that if you are presented with them you will binge. It is worth making the point here that *no food is in itself fattening*; and, conversely, that *eating too much of any food can be fattening*.

If you are still concerned that eating even a small amount of your 'forbidden' foods might make you gain weight, you might want to try a small experiment to convince yourself that this is really not the case. This experiment will involve weighing yourself more frequently than usual for a short period. If, for

DAY 1

**Breakfast:** 1 Weetabix/½ cup Wheaties with milk, orange, cup of coffee

**Mid-morning:** apple, cup of tea

**Lunch:** ham, tomato and cucumber sandwich (2 slices of bread), pack of potato chips (crisps) fruit yogurt, carton of fruit juice

**Mid-afternoon:** 2 chocolate digestive biscuits/Graham crackers, cup of tea

**Evening meal:** grilled chicken breast, 3 boiled potatoes, portion of peas, portion of carrots, glass of fruit juice, bowl of fruit salad, cup of coffee

**Bedtime:** 2 biscuits/cookies, hot chocolate drink

DAY 2

**Breakfast:** bowl cornflakes with milk, 1 slice of toast with margarine and marmalade, glass of fruit juice

**Mid-morning:** chocolate biscuit/Graham cracker, cup of tea

**Lunch:** Marmite or vegetable paté sandwich (2 slices of bread), apple, slice of fruit cake, carton of fruit juice

**Mid-afternoon:** Mars bar, cup of tea

**Evening meal:** baked potato with margarine and cheddar cheese, side salad, stewed apple, cup of coffee

**Bedtime:** scone with margarine, cup of tea

DAY 3

**Breakfast:** 2 slices of toast with margarine and marmalade, glass of fruit juice, cup of coffee

**Mid-morning:** 2 digestive biscuits/Graham crackers, cup of tea

**Lunch:** bowl of tomato soup, 2 slices of bread with margarine, cup of coffee

**Mid-afternoon:** scone with margarine, cup of tea

**Evening meal:** cod steak with cheese sauce, 2 scoops of mashed potato, portion of broccoli, 1 grilled tomato, bowl of canned or fresh fruit

**Bedtime:** slice of toast with margarine, hot chocolate drink

Figure 7   Three days of "normal" eating: an example (showing UK/US equivalents of foods where appropriate)

example, chocolate bars rank among your most difficult foods, decide to have a bar of chocolate on a particular day. Weigh yourself on that day before eating the chocolate and record your weight on your monitoring sheet. Then weigh yourself the next morning and record that weight. You will find that, contrary to your fears, eating the chocolate bar the previous day has made no difference to your weight. Acquiring this sort of concrete proof may seem silly, but can be very effective as a counterbalance to irrational but habitual and powerful fears about the fattening effects of particular foods.

You may still argue that, although one chocolate bar makes no difference to your weight and shape, you would certainly become fatter if you were to eat many of them every day. And you may be afraid that if you allowed yourself to eat any chocolate at all, you would be unable to control yourself and would eat large amounts constantly. This fear derives from your previous experience of resisting eating forbidden foods only to find that you then ate large amounts of these foods in binges. It is very important to realize that *the reason you ate large quantities of 'forbidden' food in binges was because you avoided them at other times.* The fact that you binge is not proof that you cannot control your eating; it is proof that you have been exercising inappropriate control over your eating. Although this may seem difficult to accept, if you examine your monitoring sheets you will see that it is clearly the case. The truth is that by widening your diet and getting rid of the idea of 'forbidden foods', you will be less likely to binge.

The process of widening your food choice is a difficult one and one that can easily, if things do go wrong, create more difficulty rather than less. For this reason a precise set of guidelines is specified below. It is advisable to follow this program carefully. Although this may not seem necessary to some people, there is considerable potential here for difficulty and it is not worth running unnecessary risks.

(1) Draw up a list of those foods you are avoiding either because you feel they are too 'fattening' or because you regard them as invariably, or often, triggering binges. If you find this task

difficult, take a trip to a supermarket, armed with only a pen and paper (and definitely no money), and wander around the entire shop examining the shelf contents and writing down all items you would avoid for the reasons noted above.

(2) Organize the list into a specific order or hierarchy with the item which presents the least difficulty (i.e. the one you regard as least fattening or threatening) at the bottom and the one which presents the most difficulty at the top. Figure 8 below contains an example of what such a hierarchy might

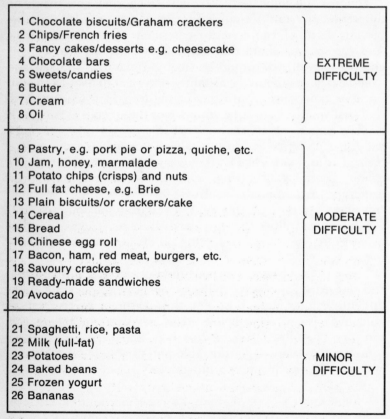

| | |
|---|---|
| 1 Chocolate biscuits/Graham crackers<br>2 Chips/French fries<br>3 Fancy cakes/desserts e.g. cheesecake<br>4 Chocolate bars<br>5 Sweets/candies<br>6 Butter<br>7 Cream<br>8 Oil | EXTREME<br>DIFFICULTY |
| 9 Pastry, e.g. pork pie or pizza, quiche, etc.<br>10 Jam, honey, marmalade<br>11 Potato chips (crisps) and nuts<br>12 Full fat cheese, e.g. Brie<br>13 Plain biscuits/or crackers/cake<br>14 Cereal<br>15 Bread<br>16 Chinese egg roll<br>17 Bacon, ham, red meat, burgers, etc.<br>18 Savoury crackers<br>19 Ready-made sandwiches<br>20 Avocado | MODERATE<br>DIFFICULTY |
| 21 Spaghetti, rice, pasta<br>22 Milk (full-fat)<br>23 Potatoes<br>24 Baked beans<br>25 Frozen yogurt<br>26 Bananas | MINOR<br>DIFFICULTY |

Figure 8    Example of a hierarchy of 'difficult' foods
(UK/US equivalents shown)

look like; but, obviously, every person's own list would be different.

(3) Divide the hierarchy into three classes of difficulty, grouping together those items that would cause you minor difficulty, those that would cause moderate difficulty, and those that would cause extreme difficulty. An example of one person's hierarchy is given in figure 8. Using the blank page which follows, create your own hierarchy of difficult foods in the way described above.

(4) Beginning with the group of foods which presents you with minor difficulty, using your established planning process, every second or third day, plan to eat one item from the list as part of your planned meals or snacks. Start with the least difficult or problematic item in the class. It is important that you plan this at a time when you feel you will be particularly safe, such as when you are eating with a friend or when it would be impossible for you to get at other food supplies. If, when the time comes, you have any doubts about whether you will be able to manage to eat the particular item without trouble ensuing, then do not eat it. If necessary, throw it away.

You should stick with the 'minor difficulty' class until you feel able to eat all the items in this category without difficulty and you feel that they ought no longer to be on your list of avoided foods. It is not possible to say how long this will take. But two or three weeks at each level is probably how long most people will need. Some will be able to move up the hierarchy more quickly and some will need to move more slowly. Once you are comfortable with the food in the first class, those items which used to present minor difficulty, you can go on to the 'moderate difficulty' class. However, it is much better to proceed with too much caution and to remain with the 'minor difficulty' class for an extra week, rather than move on when you are not really ready to do so. However long it takes, you should not move to increasingly difficult classes of food until there is nothing

## **HIERARCHY OF DIFFICULT FOODS**

you cannot eat without anxiety in the one you are tackling at present.

(5) Finally, you should, having learned that you can eat any-thing you want, decide roughly how often you would like to eat that sort of food and in what quantity. Clearly, it would be unwise to fill your day with the high-calorie and bulk food you previously ate in binges. It would also not be healthy. But it is important to remember that if you decide never to eat these foods at all they will again come to represent a threat to your control over your eating. For example, if you were avoiding chocolate, it might be sensible to decide to have a chocolate bar as 'dessert' for lunch or as a mid-afternoon snack three or four times a week. Again, if this prospect is alarming to you, it is worth reminding yourself that, if chocolate bars are the issue for you, eating three or four a week as part of controlled binge-free eating is probably a tiny fraction of the number you would be eating if you were still bingeing.

It is not possible to be precise about the length of time it will take to work through this program of eliminating dieting, because it will differ for each individual. The time taken is really not important, provided progress is being made; and progress means being able to eat a wider and wider range of food without fear. The job is done when you can eat anything, in moderation, without becoming afraid that it will cause you to get fat or to lose control and binge. If you are not sure whether you have reached this point, it might be helpful to ask yourself whether you could go out for dinner to a restaurant with a group of people, with whom you are comfortable but whom you do not know well, and order a three-course meal, or whether you could go to a dinner party with friends and eat whatever it was that was served. If you are able to say to yourself: 'Neither of these situations would present a serious problem to me because I can eat anything I like without overeating and without it making me fat,' then this particular job is done.

## Being Able to Cope in All Situations

You may be unsure how to judge the significance of the progress you have made. You may have reached the point where you can stick to your meal plan, where you no longer binge or have the urge to overeat, and where there are no foods that you cannot include in moderation in your meal plan. While this would be wonderful progress, there are two further issues which need to be addressed. One concerns your ideas and beliefs about weight and shape (see Step 6 below). The other concerns your ability to deal with all situations in which food has previously presented you with difficulty. For example, many people find it a great problem to eat food someone else has prepared and served, because they have no control over the composition, quantity or calorie content. Some people find eating in certain social situations difficult, such as at a dinner party where they feel their eating is under the public eye. It is very common for people to be quite unable to manage situations where small amounts of food keep appearing, such as cocktail parties, or where virtually limitless amounts of food are laid out, such as buffets.

To be completely secure about your eating you should come to be able to deal with any situation. The way you achieve this is by following the same principles as outlined above for being able to eat all sorts of food: you make a list of all the situations you know you would find difficult and then you practice coping in them under safe circumstances, starting with the least threatening and gradually moving on until you feel able to manage any situation in which you might find yourself.

An example of one person's list of difficult situations is shown in figure 9. In the box headed 'Difficult Situations' (p. 138) write down as many different situations as you can think of where you might experience problems in dealing with food. Then, whenever you are able to do so, try coping in the particular circumstance and make some notes about how you have managed.

---

**DIFFICULT SITUATIONS**

1 Eating nuts and savoury snacks in a bar

2 Eating in the cafeteria at work

3 Eating snacks at a cocktail party

4 Having friends over for a meal

5 Going to Sunday lunch with parents/parents-in-law

6 Going out to a dinner party

7 Having a meal at a restaurant with friends

8 Going to a buffet wedding reception

*Notes:*

---

Figure 9   Example of a list of 'difficult' situations

## **DIFFICULT SITUATIONS**

*Situation:*

*Notes:*

**REVIEW BOX 5**

Before proceeding to Step 6, ask yourself the following questions:

*Have I considered whether I have been eating enough food in my meals and snacks and, if necessary, made changes to how much I eat?*

*Have I considered which foods I avoid because they are 'dangerous', cnd instituted a program for introducing these foods into my normal eating?*

*Have I practiced eating in a range of situations which previously would have presented me with difficulty?*

If you can answer 'yes' to these questions, you should proceed to Step 6. However, Step 5 is only successfully completed when you can answer *'yes'* to the question:

*Am I able to eat in a controlled way, and in reasonable quantities, any food that I like?*

If you can answer *'yes'* to all the above questions, Step 5 has been successfully completed. However, if you can answer *'yes'* to any of the questions, you have made some progress and, while continuing working on Step 5, you can proceed to the next step.

# Step 6

# *Changing Your Mind*

It is almost certainly the case that if you had not been concerned about your weight and shape in the first place you would never have started dieting and would never have lost control of your eating and experienced all the problems that followed. In some sense, for your eating problems to be put completely behind you, *you need to change your mind about how important weight and shape are to you.* It would be quite unreasonable to say that they should become *unimportant* to you, since nearly all women in our society are concerned about their weight and shape to some extent and it is not realistic to expect you to become less concerned than is usual. However, it is important in your case that these concerns change in their intensity and their form so that they do not dominate your life and dictate how you behave, especially your eating. Clearly, this is going to be a long and difficult task. For some people, as their eating becomes increasingly 'normal', and there is space in their lives for them to develop their interests and commitments, their concerns about weight and shape naturally become increasingly less important. Others have to give special attention to changing the way they think about themselves and the importance of their shape and weight.

## Useful Books

There are a number of books which deal with the question of why weight and shape are of such major importance to women. They are mostly feminist works which expose the social pressures to be thin and the consequent tyranny under which women suffer. It is worth reading one or two of these books and considering the wider social origins of women's weight and shape concerns. Examples are Susie Orbach's *Fat is a Feminist Issue* and Naomi Wolf's *The Beauty Myth*.*

## Questioning the Importance of Weight and Shape

It is likely that, at present, how you feel about your weight and shape is central to how worthwhile you feel you are as a person. If your weight falls, you feel you are a better person. If your weight rises, you feel a failure, incompetent and unlikeable. You can judge the extent to which this is true for you by examining your monitoring sheets to see how you have felt after weighing yourself. This tendency to judge self-worth in terms of weight and shape almost always underlies eating problems. Indeed, holding these attitudes probably explains why you began dieting in the first place and why you continue to be so deeply concerned about your weight and shape.

In order to reduce the intensity of this concern, and thus make it easier for you to maintain control of your eating, it is important to reconsider the link between your self-esteem and the shape or weight of your body. One way of doing this is to make a list of the attributes which you consider valuable in other people. What things do you value about your friends, for example? Such a list might include things like how reliable and trustworthy they are, how devoted as parents they are, how dedicated to their work they are, as well as things like sense of fun, and so on. It is likely that their physical appearance, and especially their weight and shape, would rank very low on your list of valued attributes. If you are not sure about this ask yourself whether you would stop being a friend of, or start to despise, a friend if she were to gain, say, 10 pounds (while retaining all her other positive characteristics).

Another useful thing to do would be to ask a trusted friend to provide you with a list of your 'good' and 'bad' qualities, as she sees them. Again, you would almost certainly find that your weight and

* Susie Orbach, *Fat is a Feminist Issue*, London, Paddington, 1978; Naomi Wolf, *The Beauty Myth*, London, Vintage, 1991.

shape do not feature in any major way on either of these lists. Thus, it should become apparent that *weight and shape are not important in how you value others; and they are not important in how others value you.* Part of changing your mind, therefore, involves adjusting your method of self-evaluation so that you apply to yourself the same standards which you apply to others and which they apply to you. This is not achieved merely by making a decision to think differently about yourself, but the first step is to be aware of when you are giving an exaggerated importance to your weight and shape. It is useful to record on your monitoring sheets examples of instances where you attributed negative events or feelings to your weight or shape, and then enter into a kind of debate with yourself to try and reach a reasoned and rational perspective. For example, if a person to whom you are attracted does not pay much attention to you at a social gathering, you might find that you instantly think something like *'he's not interested in me because I'm too fat'.* On reflection there might be many other possible reasons why he behaved as he did, including reasons which have nothing at all to do with you. If you continue to monitor your reactions and deliberately look for other perspectives in this way you will find that gradually awareness of your weight and shape will assume a less prominent role in how you evaluate yourself and your circumstances.

## Thinking About the Way You Think

Problems with eating often arise in the context of other sorts of attitudes which are more generally problematic, and which you might usefully address. Although these will differ from person to person, two types of habitual ways of thinking seem particularly common and you might find it useful to become aware of them as potential areas of self-exploration.

*Perfectionism*
This is a tendency to have unrealistically high expectations of yourself. You might find that over the years you have, consciously or not, developed a set of rules for yourself about how to behave or how to be as a person, and that you are particularly hard on

yourself when it comes to evaluating success or failure in living up to these rules. As an example, you might think '*it is wrong to feel angry*', and then feel extremely guilty and self-critical when you do lose your temper, even in very provoking situations. Associated with this might be the tendency to be very unforgiving of yourself when you do make mistakes or fail to achieve a desired goal.

This harsh approach to your own ordinary human frailty connects with the eating problem by making you feel worse about yourself. This, in turn, makes you feel bad about your weight and shape, which makes you want to diet, which is the sure route to your binge-eating again. Changing these unrealistic expectations of yourself and such harsh self-evaluation is not easy, but it is worth trying. Again, you might begin by considering how you would evaluate a friend in similar circumstances. Would you be very critical of a friend for losing her temper in provoking circumstances, as in the example mentioned above? Would you condemn a friend for making a mistake? In any situation where you feel guilty or self-condemnatory, ask yourself whether you would accept or forgive similar behavior in your best friend and, if you would, try to apply the same sympathetic approach to yourself. In effect, treat yourself as you would your own best friend.

### '*All-or-nothing*' Thinking

This is a tendency to view things in absolute, 'all-or-nothing' terms. This principally affects thinking about weight and shape and about eating, but it can also affect more general aspects of life. For example, some people tend to see themselves at some times as a success and at other times as a total failure. In relation to their weight, they see themselves as either thin and attractive or fat and loathsome. They might think of a day when they ate very little as a great success and one where they ate a little more than they were happy with as a total disaster.

Thinking in this all-or-nothing, black-and-white way can lead to considerable difficulty. Seeing small deviations from what you are aiming at as catastrophic can make you feel that you might as well give up altogether. In reality, things are never this clearly black-and-white; everything falls somewhere between the two extremes, and a realistic appraisal of the true nature of your circumstances will allow you to make a reasoned response.

It is not easy to change an all-or-nothing style of thinking. However, it is possible to do so. Whenever you find yourself responding in an extreme negative way to a situation (e.g., *'This is a complete disaster'* or *'this is absolutely terrible'* or *'I am completely useless'*), use your monitoring sheets to slow yourself down. Before accepting your immediate response, consider what evidence there might be against it. You will find that there is often considerable evidence against the catastrophic or disastrous conclusion; and if you allow yourself to consider alternative conclusions, you will be in a position to move forward positively. It is helpful to use your monitoring sheets to write down these extreme negative thoughts and your reasoned responses to them.

### Attending a Discussion Group

There are a great many groups run by people with eating problems, where other such people meet to discuss their difficulties. Few people whose eating is seriously disturbed find that attending such a group is sufficient to help them overcome their problems with food. However, some people find that a group of this kind can be particularly helpful in revealing how concerns about weight and shape dominate and destroy ordinary life. It is sometimes only possible to see the nature and implications of your views when you hear someone else expressing them. It may be worth considering attending such a group with this purpose in mind. However, there is a danger of which you must be aware: many people have very strong views about why people have eating disorders and about what sort of help sufferers ought to be receiving. If you are attempting to overcome your eating problems on your own with the help of this manual, it will not help you to have your efforts undermined. Therefore, before you commit yourself to attending such a group it would be prudent to try to find out exactly what sort of group it is and what its purpose is. Information about groups can be obtained from eating disorders associations (see the list of addresses and telephone numbers given in Appendix 1).

## Lapses and Slippages

For people who overcome their problems with eating and resume 'normal' eating habits, disruption to the re-established control over eating is always a possibility. So, after a year of normal eating, you might find, for example, that after having had an argument with your mother or your partner, or after a particularly stressful period at work, suddenly, out of the blue, you lose control of your eating and binge. Another way that control is sometimes lost is when, for a variety of possible reasons, people gradually slip back into dieting; their weight may fall, and suddenly they binge.

This can be very distressing and invariably the immediate conclusion drawn by the person is that she is back to square one. However, this is not so. The important thing to remember is that the significance of such a lapse (and a lapse is all that it is) has less to do with what actually happens than with how you react to it. So, if you react as if struck down by a catastrophe and go into a deep depression resigning yourself to a lifetime of binge-eating, you may well find it very difficult to restore order to your eating habits. If, on the other hand, you are able to see that there were special circumstances that led to the lapse and that it represents an unfortunate minor setback which you have the skills and the will to overcome, you will be able to get back on the track of normal eating quite quickly. If you are at all concerned and feel at all vulnerable to overeating, you should immediately go back to the beginning: reinstate monitoring, specify a precise meal plan, plan your eating ahead of time, and so on. You will find after a few days of such effort that your confidence will return and you will again be able to be more relaxed about your eating.

Once your eating is under control it is enormously tempting to say to yourself. *'Thank goodness that is over. Now I need never worry about my eating again.'* This is a very natural and understandable reaction. However, it is one of which you should be wary. The concerns about your weight and shape which were the driving force in your eating disorder, even if they seem to have disappeared, remain an area of vulnerability in your life. So, at times of stress, when others in the same circumstances might

146

become depressed or anxious or drink too heavily, you are liable to become concerned about your weight and shape and to want to diet. It is important that you are alert to such feelings and take steps to avoid acting on them. Indeed, if such concerns do arise you should treat them as a problem which needs to be dealt with formally (as described in Step 5). The danger signals to which you should be particularly alert are feeling badly about yourself because of dissatisfaction with your weight and shape, and the desire to diet.

---

**REVIEW BOX 6**

Before deciding that you no longer need this manual because you consider yourself to have recovered, ask yourself the following questions.

*Am I able to eat normally without worrying about the impact on my weight and shape?*

*Am I able to eat normally without strictly planning ahead and without keeping records?*

*Am I able to accept my own worth as a human being without this depending on my view of my weight and shape?*

If you can answer 'yes' to these questions, it is safe to free yourself from the constraints of this manual and to begin to be more relaxed about your eating. However, *should you experience any difficulty in the future you should immediately put yourself back in 'treatment' and return to strict use of all the principles you have so effectively employed.*

---

# Appendix 1

# *Useful Addresses*

Should you wish to obtain information on the clinical services for eating disorders in your area, or about self-help groups, the following organizations will be able to help you:

*Great Britain*
The Eating Disorders Association
Sackville Place
44 Magdalen Street
Norwich, UK
Tel. (01603) 621414


*Australia*
The Anorexia and Bulimia Nervosa Foundation
1513 High Street
Glen Iris
3146 Victoria, Australia
Tel. (613) 885 0318


*Canada*
Bulimia Anorexia Nervosa Association
c/o Psychological Service
University of Windsor
Ontario, Canada N9B 3PH
Tel. (519) 253–7421/(519) 253–7545

*New Zealand*
Women with Eating Disorders Resource Centre
PO Box 4520
Armagh and Montreal Street
Christchurch, New Zealand
Tel. (643) 366 7725

*USA*
National Eating Disorders Organization (NEDO)
445 E. Granville Rd.
Worthington. OH 43085-3195
614-436-1112

National Association of Anorexia Nervosa and
Associated Disorders
(ANAD)
Box 7
Highland Park. IL 60035
708-831-3438

# Appendix 2

# A Note for Helpers and Advocates

You will have been asked by someone with bulimia nervosa or a related problem to help them use the self-help manual in this book to overcome their problems with eating. This appendix sketches out some general principles about how you might best be able to fulfil this function.

At the outset it is worth saying that the self-help manual has been used to considerable benefit by a great many people with bulimia nervosa. It is therefore a perfectly reasonable expectation that using this manual will be beneficial. However, the self-help program contained in this manual is obviously not the right way to proceed for everyone. In the introduction to the manual a list is provided of people for whom the manual is not appropriate. Before proceeding to help someone work through the manual you should consult this list and consider whether self-help is indeed the appropriate course of action. If you feel that it is not, clearly you must discuss this with the person you are trying to help and together you must come to a decision about the most appropriate way to proceed.

In order to help someone use this manual you should obviously be familiar with its contents. This does not mean that you must be an expert in the treatment of eating disorders. However, the self-help program follows certain definite principles in a highly structured fashion and a basic familiarity with these principles is necessary. In fact, the manual is divided into relatively small sections and it would be possible, when meeting someone you are helping, to skim through reasonably quickly the section with which they are currently concerned.

A *Self-Help Manual*

The most useful function that you can perform is to provide basic support and encouragement. There are bound to be times when someone trying to deal with her eating problems feels discouraged and even hopeless about ever effecting a significant change. It is at these times that the balanced perspective of an outsider can be most useful. When all one can see is one's failures, it can be immensely reassuring and helpful to be reminded of the successes one has had and the progress one has made.

It is important to emphasize that the manual is a guide to *self*-help; and if you are assisting someone in their use of this manual then you are helping her to help herself. So it is not your role to devise plans and strategies for her, but rather to encourage her to develop her own techniques for overcoming her difficulties. This does not mean, of course, that you should refuse to make any suggestions at all. There are times when, by looking through someone's monitoring sheets, certain patterns she has missed are obvious to an outsider. If you spot anything you feel might be important then obviously you should raise it. Similarly, certain points of detail, concerning, for example, the sort of food eaten or the timing of meals, may well seem to you worth mentioning and it is perfectly reasonable to do so. However, while you should feel free to make suggestions about prudent courses of action, in the end it is those strategies which the person generates for herself which she is most likely to follow and which are therefore likely to be of most benefit to her. And, of course, in the end the responsibility to use whatever points you make is hers and not yours.

Overcoming bulimia nervosa is a struggle which will take many months. In the early stages of this self-help program it would be useful for the person using the manual to be able to see her helper often. Weekly sessions are usually advisable at this stage. Once some control over eating has been achieved, such frequent sessions may not be needed. Sessions every two weeks are then sufficient for a few months, after which meetings can become less and less frequent. However, it is important that the door is left open for help. This is especially important at times when someone who has been doing well experiences a lapse. If left entirely on her own she can become so disheartened that she gives up altogether, and what was really a minor lapse becomes a relapse. This is unnecessary; a couple of booster sessions with a helper/advocate is usually sufficient to get the person back on the course to recovery.

Deciding to recruit such a helper and make a genuine effort to use this manual to overcome eating problems is a brave decision. Anyone making that decision deserves a great deal of respect, support and encouragement. And with such help, she stands a good chance of making substantial improvement.

# Appendix 3

# *The Views of Users*

If you are having doubts about whether the manual would work for you, it would be helpful to talk to one or two people who have used it. Certainly, if you can find such people, such discussion could only be beneficial. However, short of making a very public declaration about your difficulties, it may be very difficult if not impossible to make the appropriate contacts. As a substitute for this, four people who have used the manual have written brief accounts which are included below.

1)
'*I was in a very bad way. I had developed anorexia at the age of thirteen. After about three years of eating virtually nothing I found that I began to lose control. It was then that I started making myself sick to get rid of food I shouldn't have eaten. Soon I was having full blown binges. After a year of this I had got into a routine of making myself sick repeatedly all day. This would happen anything up to ten times a day. I never went out and had lost all interest in life. I had given up hope of ever getting better and really felt that I would carry on binge-eating until it killed me.*

*When I first read the manual I have to admit that I was rather dubious. I was willing to give anything a go but I really thought that it would take a lot more than a book to make me better. But the moment I started working through the manual I started improving. Even though to begin with even controlling breakfast for one day seemed impossible, I gave it a go and to my surprise I found that there were things I could do to help. I took things very* slowly, but as I began gaining confidence that planning meals wouldn't make me any fatter (a very big worry for me) I began to find things easier. The hardest thing was to get back on the plan after I had binged. I felt that if I wasn't sick or didn't starve myself I would definitely get fat and that made me feel very scared. But I stuck at it and eventually I found that if things went wrong, even if I binged, this wouldn't in itself make me fat and that to go back on the plan, rather than a route to fatness, was an insurance against binge-eating again.

The most difficult part of the manual for me was trying not to count calories and diet. I know the calorie content of just about every type of food there is and I used to weigh myself after every significant event (eating, not eating, vomiting, not vomiting, etc.). But I tried really hard and I am much better now. I still often feel like weighing myself and I still find that almost unconsciously I am counting up calories, but I try really hard not to let this affect what I am doing – and almost always now I succeed! Increasing my overall calorie intake and introducing new foods was terribly difficult. It still sometimes worries me and I do occasionally feel guilty if I eat some things. But I am a lot better now and can eat most things fairly comfortably.

The manual gave me confidence and hope as well as practical advice. Although I have not had a full binge in a long time (and I haven't vomited in almost two years), I still follow the principals of the manual. So most days I very loosely plan what to eat. And if I feel shaky for a day or two, even though I don't think I will binge again, I write out a plan just to give me more confidence.

My life has improved enormously. Looking back I can't believe I ever lived the way I did or was as unhappy as I was.'

2)
'One of my difficulties deciding to do something to change was that it seemed so self-indulgent. After all, lots of people have all sorts of problems and they just have to get on with their lives. But the truth I had to face was that my problem with eating was much more invasive than I wished to pretend – it affected everything and I just couldn't be _me_ while I still had the problem. It was the pregnancy that brought it home to me. I tried really hard to eat

sensibly, and things did at first improve in that I did binge less and I did stop vomiting and taking laxatives the moment I found out I was pregnant. But, in truth, my eating habits remained atrocious. Food was always on my mind, dominating my every waking minute. Even my dreams centered on food. I was desperately anxious not to put on too much weight and tried to keep a tight check on what I ate, calorie counting and trying to keep under 1500 calories a day. I also did a lot of exercise. I knew that there was a danger that some of the things I was doing would not be good for the baby and that is what brought it home to me that I had to do something to change the way I was.

I read the self-help program right through from beginning to end in one sitting. I knew immediately that it made sense. Although there was quite a lot in it which I didn't like and which, quite honestly, made me pretty scared, I had reached such a low ebb on my own that I knew there was just no point in continuing to fool myself that I could get back to a normal life without doing a lot of things I really didn't want to do. What impressed me most about the program was that it didn't say 'eat this' and 'don't eat that', but rather it explained how to get on the right track in a realistic straightforward way. I felt confidence in it because it understood my problem. I have read a lot of books about eating problems and this is the first time that I have had that feeling. Of course, having sunk so low I was in exactly the right frame of mind when I read the book, but it was exactly what I needed.

I was very meticulous about working through the program. Having had problems with my eating for over fifteen years, I did not mind going slowly because I could see right at the beginning that I was making progress. I spent a few months 'eliminating dieting'. I suppose in some ways I am still working at it. This was the hardest part of all but it feels to me now as if it was the most important. I am glad I took it so slowly.

Even now, when my eating has been fine for over a year, I still carry the book around with me wherever I go. And occasionally, I go back to particular bits I have underlined and found especially helpful just to reassure myself. In a sense, changing my eating pattern was not really that difficult once I had made up my mind to follow the steps religiously. What has been much more difficult is *changing me – or, as the book puts it, changing my mind. I have wasted so much of my life worrying about how much I weigh and how fat I am and it is not a simple thing to just stop doing this. I am much, much better. But I do still have my moments. I have taken to talking to myself rather a lot. My mother used to joke that this is the first sign of madness. But in my case, although I do sometimes feel a bit silly, it is definitely a route to sanity. Essentially what I do is argue myself out of ways of thinking about myself which have caused me nothing but trouble. And it is working. There is so much I can do now without anxiety that would have been unimaginable a few years ago. The best of it is what this means for my family. We take our baby swimming together, we go out for meals, we can do anything.*

*So I am really glad that I resisted all the excuses I used to come up with for not tackling my eating problems. I have never done a better thing in my life.'*

3)
*'It was only when I hit rock bottom that I went to my doctor to ask for help. For almost ten years my life had been totally dominated by food and I had reached the point of utter desperation.*

*My first impression of the manual was utter disbelief. I had come for help to be thin and what I was being told was that the way not to feel fat was to eat! But I had long since run out of any ideas of my own and I had to do something so I decided to give it a try. At first it was terribly difficult. Every day there were setbacks and on some days it was the same old routine of binge or starve. By talking to my friends about my problems for the first time the steps in the book became clearer and somehow achievable. I have to say that there were several points at which, if I had not had such supportive friends, I think I would probably have given up altogether. Learning to eat 'normally' is not easy when you have no concept of 'normal'. But each step was a goal to achieve and, once achieved, something to build on. Eating properly itself reduced the hunger and the panic attacks. And, as I learned to eat regularly so I found less need to binge and starve. And then, after what must have been some months, suddenly I began to believe in myself and everything suddenly became much easier. I began to dissociate weight and size from my feelings about myself. Surprisingly, I even began to look better: my hair shone and my skin was clear. I'd lost that dull heavy feeling inside and for the first time in years I believed that happiness was possible.*

*Nearly two years on I am a completely new person. It has taken some time to reach this point and for the person wanting instant results the realization that the struggle will be a long one is a hard one to take. But it is worth it. Every day now I am realizing what has changed. Only the other day I stood in the same supermarket that used to fill me with dread holding a basket with real food in it – by which I mean a combination of fruit, vegetables, breakfast cereal, pasta and even a pack of crackers (to last a whole week this time and not just five minutes).*

*It took a few months of using the manual to really feel the results. The hardest part is that you have to believe in something that seems so contradictory to your own bulimic reasoning. Everyone has commented on the changes in me. Even people who have no idea about the problems I had can see that something positive has happened. For the first time in my life I can honestly say that I feel attractive, loveable and of worth. I never believed I would be able to say that.'*

4)
*'I am twenty-one and I have been fighting against bulimia nervosa for six years. It has blighted my enjoyment of life and there have been numerous occasions and thousands of hours of utter desperation. I cannot now remember how it feels not to have my partner in crime, "bulimia", by my side, inside me, making a mockery of me and my urgent desire to gain some control over my life. But now there is light at the end of the tunnel. By using the manual I have become stronger and more determined and I can see that it is possible to defeat this illness which, in the past, ruled my existence and was so damaging to my youth and potential love of life.*

*I had had counselling when I was seventeen, but it wasn't really any help. Then, a year ago, I went for counselling again because I had reached an all time low and was engulfed by a sense of total inadequacy. I was hungry, tired and emotionally empty – the ideal circumstances for bulimia to thrive upon. Fortunately, I was given* the manual. It was (and still is) invaluable. What was especially important for me was that it did not attempt to solve the problems of bulimia for me. It didn't patronise me, which would have been both arrogant and pointless. Instead, the first thing it did for me was to inform me with knowledge about the disorder. By giving me convincing explanations for my behavior, it made me realize that my actions were not freakish but common to this disorder. It equipped me with a greater understanding of all aspects of the problem of bulimia, and I could therefore challenge it from a position of strength.

I had been told for years all the correct attitudes that I ought to have until I was blue in the face, but it did no good, because for six years my body and my mind were so unbalanced by my irregular eating habits and the punishment I put myself through. Consequently, however hard I have tried to adopt sane, normal beliefs on the priority of weight and shape in my life and with what I equate success, my warped perspective remained dominant. This has now changed. The manual helped me so much by giving me, on a day-to-day basis, practical and realistic strategies and goals. I think it is absolutely right that it leaves the psychological aspects until the end of the program because, from my own experience, it is only then, when your eating is stable, that you are equipped to think about actually reprioritizing, about changing the way you think. This process has to be self-initiated to succeed in the long term and you need to be ready to take these steps.

For me one thing that has been really important has been the availability of the manual. I can refer to it privately as a confidante, as a friend, whenever necessary. It is a reminder of the truthful facts when I lose sight and when I feel I am slipping back. I have turned the corner now and, by continuing with the manual, I know I will be all right. After all these years this is hard to believe.'